Preface

This collection of papers draws together a variety of approaches for adding object orientation to the Z formal specification language. These papers are not a conference proceedings, but have a slightly more complicated history.

This work has grown and evolved from some work originally done in the ZIP project, under the United Kingdom's Department of Trade and Industry (DTI) IED initiative. ZIP is a three year project which aims to make the use of the Z specification language more widespread. It hopes to achieve this by producing a standard for Z; developing a method for Z; building tool support for Z; and carrying out research into refinement, proof and concurrency in Z.

The ZIP methods work includes performing a survey of current Z practitioners (reported in [Barden *et al.* 1992]); investigating current styles and methods of Z usage; and developing a Z Method handbook (available early in 1993). As part of this work, we carried out a comparative study of the ways in which object orientation has been combined with Z. A summary of that work has been published as [Stepney *et al.* 1992].

In the Summer of 1991, the ZOOM workshop was held at Lady Margaret Hall, Oxford, organized and funded by the Z User Group. At this workshop, various parties interested in combining object orientation and Z formal specifications got together. There are no published proceedings, but the discussions are reported in [Carrington 1992]. As part of the material supplied to participants, a copy of the ZIP comparative study was distributed. When proponents of other 'object oriented Z' approaches saw the document, they expressed interest in having their own methods represented.

Consequently, a new document was prepared, structured as a series of 'authored chapters'. This was distributed to participants at the 6th Annual Z User meeting, held at the University of York in December 1991. The new document was well received, and Springer-Verlag agreed to publish a revised version in their 'Workshops in Computing' series. For this version, many chapters have been substantially revised, and a new chapter describing a further approach has been added.

We would like to thank all the authors of the various chapters, without whose enthusiasm and hard work this book would not have been possible. We would also like to thank Anthony Hall, Brian Hepworth, Trevor King and David Pitt for their help. The part funding by the DTI for ZIP (project number IED4/1/1639) is gratefully acknowledged.

May 1992   Susan Stepney, Rosalind Barden and David Cooper

Contents

1

Why an Object Oriented Z?

1.1 Introduction

Z is one of the more popular formal specification languages [Spivey 1989], [Hayes 1987], [Potter *et al.* 1991]. It makes use of *schemas* to structure specifications [Woodcock 1989]. But the message coming from many users is that the Z schema is not sufficient for structuring large specifications [Barden *et al.* 1992]. Many groups of workers are proposing their own extensions to provide various degrees of modularity. Initially, these proposals were based on simple textual devices, such as formal chapters with facilities including import and export statements, generic parameters, and library chapters [Flynn *et al.* 1990], [Sampaio and Meira 1990]. These are a start, but something more sophisticated is needed.

Rather than inventing something from scratch, what can be learnt from advances in software structuring techniques? Object orientation is a technology that offers much promise as a means for structuring large, complex software systems [Meyer 1988], [Cox 1986], [Booch 1991]. It has overcome the common hype phase to become an approach that is being taken up and used for significant software development.

'Object oriented' means different things to different people. Section 1.2 summarizes some of the more standard definitions, and section 1.3 explains why Z as it stands cannot be described as object oriented.

The papers collected here describe many different proposed approaches for providing Z with an object oriented structuring mechanism. These include attempts to use Z in a more object oriented style, and proposed extensions to Z to allow fully object oriented specifications. The approaches covered here are:

- Z in an OO style

    3. Hall's style [Hall 1990], [Brownbridge 1990]
    4. ZERO [Whysall and McDermid 1991a], [Whysall and McDermid 1991b]

- OO extensions to Z

    5. MooZ [Meira and Cavalcanti 1991]
    6. Object-Z [Duke *et al.* 1991]
    7. OOZE [Alencar and Goguen 1991]
    8. Schuman & Pitt [Schuman and Pitt 1987], [Schuman *et al.* 1990]

---

9. Z^{++} [Lano 1991]
10. ZEST [Cusack 1991]

When a new approach is first being described, it is often used to specify examples chosen to highlight its novel and interesting features. But this makes it be difficult to evaluate the alternatives, as there is no common ground for a direct comparison. For this reason, in this collection, each approach has been used to specify the same two problems.

So each chapter follows the same format. First, the particular approach is described. Then it is used to specify a simple example (section 2.2): that of quadrilaterals, with special cases of parallelograms, rhombi, rectangles and squares, along with various operations on them such as 'move' and 'rotate', as might be required by a simple drawing package. Finally, a larger specification is given (section 2.3), to enable a fuller comparison and evaluation. This is a specification of various button icons that could be part of a user interface design, including the specification of how different sorts of buttons react to mouse events.

Z is not the only formal specification language being provided with object oriented extensions. For example, Fresco [Wills 1991] is based on VDM. Chapter 11 has been included to allow a further comparison.

Work has also been done on marrying Z and HOOD (an object-based design notation for Ada) [Giovanni and Iachini 1990], [Iachini 1991]. This is summarized in appendix A.

1.2   What is 'object oriented'?

In order to explain why Z is not object oriented, we need to define what we mean by 'object oriented'. To do this, we consider Booch's definitions of objects [Booch 1991], and Wegner's classification scheme [Wegner 1987b].

1.2.1   Booch's definitions

Booch provides definitions of 'object' and 'class'. (The page numbers below refer to [Booch 1991].)

"An object has state, exhibits some well-defined behaviour, and has a unique identity." [page 77]

"The state of an object encompasses all of the (usually static) properties of the object plus the current (usually dynamic) values of each of these properties." [page 78]

"Behaviour is how an object acts and reacts, in terms of state changes and message passing." [page 80]

"Identity is that property of an object which distinguishes it from all other objects." [page 84]

"a message is ... an operation one object performs upon another" [page 80]

The definition of message is a little different from the conventional one: it is more usual to say that an object's behaviour is defined in terms of its operations (or methods), and that another object sends a message *requesting* the execution of an operation. In other words, objects are not thought of as performing operations on other objects, rather they perform operations on themselves, in response to requests. This terminology better emphasizes objects' autonomy.

Booch defines a class to be the abstraction mechanism:

"the structure and behaviour of similar objects are defined in their common class" [page 77]

"A class is a set of objects that share a common structure and a common behaviour." [page 93]

"A single object is ... an instance of a class." [page 93]

These definitions are a little difficult to reconcile: is a class the set of all its actual instances, or of all its potential instances, or is it a description (abstraction) of the commonality of its instances?

1.2.2   Wegner's classification

Wegner provides a classification scheme for languages: object based, class based and object oriented. (The page numbers below refer to [Wegner 1987a].)

"An object has a set of 'operations' and a 'state' that remembers the effect of the operations." [page 168]

Wegner, unlike Booch, does not explicitly mention identity.

"A language is object-based if it supports objects as a language feature." [page 169]

Although Z can be used to specify state and operations by using schemas, it does not actually 'support objects as a language feature', and so cannot truly be called even object based by this definition. However, if the definition is interpreted sufficiently loosely, the fact that Z supports a 'state and operations' style of specification can be used to say it does in some sense support objects.

"A class is a template ... from which objects may be created by 'create' or 'new' operations. Objects of the same class have common operations and therefore uniform behaviour." [page 169]

Since 'operation' hasn't been defined, it is not possible to deduce whether operations are applicable only to objects (that is, whether they are what are usually called 'methods'). If 'new' or 'create' are methods, it implies classes are objects, as is done in Smalltalk [Goldberg and Robson 1983], with all the associated problems this has. However, the definition certainly implies that a class is not some sort of 'collection of all objects', but is a process that outputs objects. Wegner nowhere uses the conventional phrase 'an object is an instance of a class'.

"A class may inherit operations from 'superclasses' and may have its operations inherited by 'subclasses'. An object of the class C ... has C as its 'base class' and may use operations defined in its base class as well as operations defined in superclasses." [page 169]

[Wegner 1987a], [Wegner 1987b] goes on to identify two kinds of inheritance. With strict inheritance (defined above), descendants are behaviourally compatible with their ancestors. This is also called the *is-a* relation: a dog is-a mammal, etc. The definition ought also to say an object *must* be able to use operations of its superclasses, in order that it can be used 'in place of' any object higher up the hierarchy. Non-strict inheritance captures the notion of similarity rather than compatibility, and operations can been modified or removed. This is also called the *like* relation: an emu is like a bird, but it can't fly, etc.

The fact that the state cannot be hidden in Z is not a problem (as far as Wegner's definitions go); data abstraction is a separate, orthogonal feature:

"A data abstraction is an object whose state is accessible only through its operations." [page 170]

Wegner's definition of a fully object oriented language is

"An object-based language is object-oriented if its objects belong to classes and class hierarchies may be incrementally defined by an inheritance mechanism." [page 169]

1.3   Z is not object oriented

Z can be used to specify a state (via a schema) and behaviour (as operation schemas). However, Z does not support the grouping of operations on a particular state (except possibly textually), the application of these operations to different instances, or inheritance of these properties.

Using Wegner's classification, we can say (in the letter, if not the spirit, of the definitions) that Z is object based (it 'supports' objects), but certainly it is not object *oriented*.

1.4   Philosophical aside

Objects are physical, concrete things which exist in the 'real' world, the classes they belong to are abstractions we build, and do not have their own existence. You can sit on a particular chair, but you cannot sit on, or even point to, an abstraction common to all chairs: the class of all chairs[1]. Even more abstract are

---

[1] This view is not undisputed. The Platonic view gives a greater reality to an abstract class than to its imperfect instances, because we perceive the 'real' world only through a filter.

the hierarchies we places these classes in. The class of chairs could occur in a hierarchy along with the class of tables, both below the class of furniture — but this hierarchy of abstractions also has no concrete existence of its own.

Since it is we who choose the classes and hierarchies, which have no independent existence, it is not surprising, and we should not worry, that sometimes the questions 'which class does this object belong to?' or 'where do these classes fit in the hierarchy?' have poorly defined answers. There is a further point: although objects have their own existence, again it is we who choose where the boundary between object and not-object is drawn; this boundary also has no existence in its own right. So even the question 'is this an object?' can have a poorly defined answer.

We choose how to divide the world into discrete objects, how to group objects we think are alike into classes, and how to arrange classes in hierarchies based on similarities we perceive. In each case we could make a different choice. This should be seen as an opportunity, not as a problem: we can choose the classifications to suit ourselves, in order to simplify the model we are trying to build, to make the problem we are trying to solve easier.

There is 'no one right way' to do the modelling; some choices will be better for some aspects of the problem, other choices better for other aspects, but probably no choice will be best for all aspects. [Peterson 1988] sums up well what we should be looking for in the models we build when he says: *The idea is not to paint a realistic portrait but to capture the spirit of the phenomenon with a caricature.*

2

Example Specifications in Z

2.1 Introduction

The current Z reference work is [Spivey 1989]. Several Z case studies can be found in [Hayes 1987]. A tutorial introduction to Z is given in [Potter *et al.* 1991].

2.2 Quadrilaterals Example

This section details the small example chosen to introduce each of the identified approaches. The specification chosen is that of different sorts of quadrilaterals, as may be needed for a drawing package. It is the basis for the various respecifications in object oriented Z styles in the following chapters.

2.2.1 Class Hierarchy

The classes are *Quadrilateral*, *Parallelogram* (derived from *Quadrilateral*), *Rhombus* and *Rectangle* (both derived from *Parallelogram*), and *Square* (derived from both *Rhombus* and *Rectangle*).

The desired class hierarchy consists of

- *Quadrilateral*: a general four-sided figure
- *Parallelogram*: a *Quadrilateral* that has opposite sides parallel
- *Rhombus*: a *Parallelogram* with all sides the same length
- *Rectangle*: a *Parallelogram* with perpendicular sides
- *Square*: both a *Rectangle* and a *Rhombus*

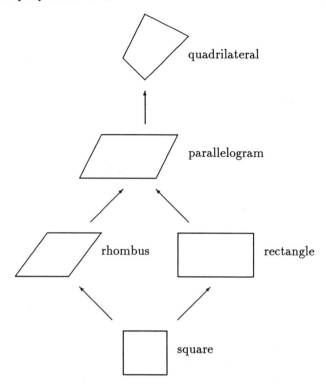

quadrilateral

parallelogram

rhombus

rectangle

square

2.2.2   Vectors and Scalars

Vectors are used to specify the quadrilaterals. Their components, length, and so on, are of type *Scalar*, which is not further defined (it could be implemented as a real number, or as an integer, or even symbolically to allow accurate scaling and so on).

$$[\mathit{Vector}, \mathit{Scalar}]$$

The vector operations addition, modulus and dot product are used. They have their conventional definitions.

$$
\begin{array}{|l}
\_ + \_ : \mathit{Vector} \times \mathit{Vector} \rightarrow \mathit{Vector} \\
| \_ | : \mathit{Vector} \rightarrow \mathit{Scalar} \\
\_ . \_ : \mathit{Vector} \times \mathit{Vector} \rightarrow \mathit{Scalar} \\
\hline
\text{(definitions omitted)}
\end{array}
$$

2.2.3   Edges

The edges of a general four sided figure are specified by four vectors:

$$
\begin{array}{|l}
\underline{\mathit{Edges}} \underline{} \\
v1, v2, v3, v4 : \mathit{Vector} \\
\hline
v1 + v2 + v3 + v4 = 0
\end{array}
$$

One of the vectors is redundant: the invariant shows that the vectors representing the four edges sum to zero.

Five kinds of quadrilateral, distinguished by stronger constraints on their edges, are distinguished:

$$EdgeKind ::= Quadrilateral$$
$$| \quad Parallelogram$$
$$| \quad Rhombus$$
$$| \quad Rectangle$$
$$| \quad Square$$

Each of these kinds puts a constraint on the allowed edges.

A *Quadrilateral* has no further constraints on its edges. Notice this definition allows edges to cross, or be zero. If this is not desired, a stronger constraint should be used.

A *Parallelogram* has opposite *Edges* equal in length and opposite in direction.

```
┌─ IsaParallelogram ──────────────────────────────────
│ edges : Edges
├──────────────────────────────────────────────────────
│ edges.v1 + edges.v3 = 0
└──────────────────────────────────────────────────────
```

A *Rhombus* is a *Parallelogram* that also has adjacent sides of the same length.

```
┌─ IsaRhombus ────────────────────────────────────────
│ edges : Edges
├──────────────────────────────────────────────────────
│ IsaParallelogram
│ | edges.v1 |=| edges.v2 |
└──────────────────────────────────────────────────────
```

A *Rectangle* is a *Parallelogram* that also has perpendicular adjacent sides.

```
┌─ IsaRectangle ──────────────────────────────────────
│ edges : Edges
├──────────────────────────────────────────────────────
│ IsaParallelogram
│ (edges.v1).(edges.v2) = 0
└──────────────────────────────────────────────────────
```

A *Square* is a *Rhombus* and a *Rectangle*.

```
┌─ IsaSquare ─────────────────────────────────────────
│ edges : Edges
├──────────────────────────────────────────────────────
│ IsaRhombus
│ IsaRectangle
└──────────────────────────────────────────────────────
```

2.2.4   A Quadrilateral

For a drawing package, the position of the quadrilateral is also needed. So a general quadrilateral is specified by its edges, its position and its kind.

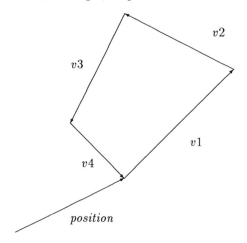

```
┌─ Quad ─────────────────────────────────────────────────
│ edges : Edges
│ position : Vector
│ kind : EdgeKind
├────────────────────────────────────────────────────────
│ (      kind = Parallelogram ∧ IsaParallelogram
│ ∨      kind = Rhombus ∧ IsaRhombus
│ ∨      kind = Rectangle ∧ IsaRectangle
│ ∨      kind = Square ∧ IsaSquare)
└────────────────────────────────────────────────────────
```

The predicate ensures that the edges and kind of the quadrilateral are consistent

2.2.5   Operations on a Quadrilateral

2.2.5.1   Moving the Quadrilateral

A quadrilateral can be moved (translated) by changing its position component:

```
┌─ MoveQuad ─────────────────────────────────────────────
│ Δ Quad
│ move? : Vector
├────────────────────────────────────────────────────────
│ edges' = edges
│ position' = position + move?
│ kind' = kind
└────────────────────────────────────────────────────────
```

2.2.5.2   Querying the Angle between two Edges

For all except general quadrilaterals, the angle between two adjacent sides is well defined: there are only two different angles and the second is π minus the first.

[*Angle*]

$$\cos^{-1} : Scalar \nrightarrow Angle$$
$$\_/\_ : Scalar \times Scalar \nrightarrow Scalar$$

(definitions omitted)

AngleQuad
$\Xi Quad$
$a! : Angle$

$kind \in \{Parallelogram, Rhombus\}$
$$\wedge \; a! = \cos^{-1}\left(\frac{(edges.v1).(edges.v2)}{\mid edges.v1 \mid \mid edges.v2 \mid}\right)$$
$\vee$
$kind \in \{Rectangle, Square\} \wedge a! = \pi/2$

The separate predicate for squares and rectangles is not strictly necessary — it is a consequence of the other definition and the predicate on edges — but it is put in explicitly to emphasize this fact.

2.2.5.3 Shearing the Quadrilateral

Shearing the quadrilateral makes sense for all except squares, rhombi and rectangles, since the process does not maintain their invariants.

[*Shear*]

ShearQuad
$\Delta Quad$
$s? : Shear$

$kind \in \{Quadrilateral, Parallelogram\} \wedge$
(rest of definition omitted)

Notice that it is not strictly necessary to put in the test for the quad kind, since it would be impossible to satisfy both the shear and edge conditions for the other kinds (except for the null shear).

2.2.6 A Drawing System

The state of the drawing system consists of a mapping from quadrilateral identifiers to quadrilaterals:

[*QID*]

DrawingSystem
$screen : QID \nrightarrow Quad$

2.2.6.1   Adding and Deleting a Quadrilateral

The operation *AddQuad* adds a quadrilateral to the *DrawingSystem*.

```
┌─ AddQuad ─────────────────────────────────────────
│ ΔDrawingSystem
│ q? : Quad
├───────────────────────────────────────────────────
│ ∃ qid' : QID | qid' ∉ dom screen •
│     screen' = screen ∪ {qid' ↦ q?}
└───────────────────────────────────────────────────
```

The operation *DeleteQuad* deletes a quadrilateral from the *DrawingSystem*.

```
┌─ DeleteQuad ──────────────────────────────────────
│ ΔDrawingSystem
│ qid? : QID
├───────────────────────────────────────────────────
│ qid? ∈ dom screen
│ screen' = {qid?} ◁ screen
└───────────────────────────────────────────────────
```

2.2.6.2   Promoting the Operations

First, we define a general updating schema, which performs an, as yet unspecified, change to a particular *Quad* in the drawing system:

```
┌─ ΦUpdateDS ───────────────────────────────────────
│ ΔDrawingSystem
│ ΔQuad
│ qid? : QID
├───────────────────────────────────────────────────
│ qid? ∈ dom screen
│ θQuad = screen qid?
│ screen' = screen ⊕ {qid? ↦ θQuad'}
└───────────────────────────────────────────────────
```

The operations on an individual quadrilateral can be promoted to operations on a quadrilateral in the drawing system:

$$MoveDS \mathrel{\widehat{=}} (\Phi UpdateDS \wedge MoveQuad) \setminus \Delta Quad$$
$$AngleDS \mathrel{\widehat{=}} (\Phi UpdateDS \wedge AngleQuad) \setminus \Delta Quad$$
$$ShearDS \mathrel{\widehat{=}} (\Phi UpdateDS \wedge ShearQuad) \setminus \Delta Quad$$

2.3   Button Example

This section details the larger example chosen to evaluate each of the identified approaches. The specification chosen is that of the kind of screen buttons that can be selected by using a mouse. It is the basis for the various respecifications in object oriented Z styles in the following chapters.

2.3.1   Class Hierarchy

The class hierarchy consists of:

- a generic *Button*, used as a virtual class
- an *ActionButton*, a specialization of *Button*, which performs some actions (in object-oriented parlance, sends some messages) when selected
- an *OnOffButton*, a specialization of *Button*, which has a state (in order to be consulted later, possibly), used as a virtual class
- a *ToggleButton*, a specialization of *OnOffButton*, which toggles its state when selected
- a *RadioButton*, a specialization of *OnOffButton* and *ActionButton*, which can be switched on by the user, at which point it performs the actions of telling the associated radio buttons to switch off

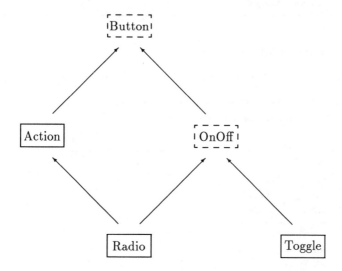

2.3.2   A Button's State

There are three kinds of buttons (the others mentioned are the equivalent of 'virtual classes', defined to factor out common properties, but never instantiated):

$$ButtonKind ::= Action \mid Toggle \mid Radio$$

The button notes the mouse's location; the mouse can be located either *In* or *Out* of the button's active area.

$$MouseLocation ::= In \mid Out$$

The mouse has one mouse button. This can be either released, *Up*, or depressed, in which case either the (screen) button is *Primed* for action (if the mouse was depressed in the button's active area), or the mouse is being *Ignored*.

$$MouseClick ::= Up \mid Primed \mid Ignored$$

Some buttons perform actions when clicked:

[*ACTION*]

Some buttons have a state that is *On* or *Off*.

Status ::= *On* | *Off*

So the button schema is:

```
__ Button _____
  kind : ButtonKind
  loc : MouseLocation
  click : MouseClick
  action : P ACTION
  status : Status
```

2.3.3   Initialization

This section describes the behaviour that all buttons have in common.

When a button is created it is told the actions and initial status, if relevant. The mouse is *Up* and not in the active area:

```
__ InitButton _____
  Button'
  kind? : ButtonKind
  act? : ACTION
  status? : Status
_____
  kind' = kind?
  loc' = Out
  click' = Up
  (        kind? = Action ∧ action' = act?
   ∨       kind? = Toggle ∧ status' = status?
   ∨       kind? = Radio ∧ action' = act? ∧ status' = status?)
```

2.3.4   Operations

Changes to the *Button*'s state never change *kind* or *action*:

```
__ ΔButton _____
  Button
  Button'
_____
  kind' = kind
  action' = action
```

There are four things the mouse can do:

- *MouseUp* : release its button
- *MouseDown* : click its button
- *MouseLeave* : leave the button's active area
- *MouseEnter* : enter the button's active area

In an implementation, such changes would cause the display of the button to change in some way, for example showing it in inverse video or with a thickened border. Such details are not specified here.

For all buttons, on *MouseUp*, the mouse location is unchanged, and the mouse click state changes to *Up*:

$$\begin{array}{|l}
\underline{\ MouseUpButton\ \rule{7cm}{0pt}} \\
\Delta Button \\
\hline
loc' = loc \\
click' = Up \\
\\
\end{array}$$

If the button is being ignored, nothing else happens (except the empty set of actions is sent: a kludge, because the *act!* value must be specified for all cases, not just when an action occurs):

$$\begin{array}{|l}
\underline{\ MouseUpIgnored\ \rule{7cm}{0pt}} \\
MouseUpButton \\
act! : \mathbf{P}\ ACTION \\
\hline
click = Ignored \\
status' = status \\
act! = \varnothing \\
\end{array}$$

A primed action button outputs its actions:

$$\begin{array}{|l}
\underline{\ MouseUpPrimedAction\ \rule{6cm}{0pt}} \\
MouseUpButton \\
act! : \mathbf{P}\ ACTION \\
\hline
kind = Action \\
click = Primed \\
act! = b.action \\
\end{array}$$

A primed toggle button changes its state (and outputs the empty action; its purpose is to note its state, possibly in order to be consulted later):

$$\begin{array}{|l}
\underline{\ MouseUpPrimedToggle\ \rule{6cm}{0pt}} \\
MouseUpButton \\
act! : \mathbf{P}\ ACTION \\
\hline
kind = Toggle \\
click = Primed \\
status' \neq status \\
act! = \varnothing \\
\end{array}$$

A primed radio button switches on and outputs its action if it is off, otherwise it does nothing, since it is already on:

```
┌─ MouseUpPrimedRadio ─────────────────────────────
│ MouseUpButton
│ act! : P ACTION
├──────────────────────────
│ kind = Radio
│ click = Primed
│ (      status = Off ∧ act! = action
│ ∨       status = On ∧ act! = ∅)
│ status' = On
└──────────────────────────────────────────────────
```

So the complete *MouseUp* specification is:

$$MouseUp \;\hat{=}\; MouseUpIgnored$$
$$\lor\; MouseUpPrimedAction$$
$$\lor\; MouseUpPrimedToggle$$
$$\lor\; MouseUpPrimedRadio$$

In the other three operations the *status*, where relevant, does not change.

```
┌─ ΔButtonSt ──────────────────────────────────────
│ ΔButton
├──────────────────────────
│ kind ∈ {Toggle, Radio} ⇒ status' = status
└──────────────────────────────────────────────────
```

If the *MouseDown* occurs while the mouse is *In* the button's active area, then the button becomes *Primed*, otherwise the mouse is *Ignored*.

```
┌─ MouseDown ──────────────────────────────────────
│ ΔButtonSt
├──────────────────────────
│ loc' = loc
│ (      loc = In ∧ click' = Primed
│ ∨      loc = Out ∧ click' = Ignored)
└──────────────────────────────────────────────────
```

MouseLeave and *MouseEnter* change only the location:

```
┌─ MouseLeave ─────────────────────────────────────
│ ΔButtonSt
├──────────────────────────
│ loc' = Out
│ click' = click
└──────────────────────────────────────────────────
```

```
┌─ MouseEnter ─────────────────────────────────────
│ ΔButtonSt
├──────────────────────────
│ loc' = In
│ click' = click
└──────────────────────────────────────────────────
```

A radio button that is on may be asked to turn off (if one of the others in its group has sent it a message to turn on):

```
┌─ TurnOff ─────────────────────────────────────────
│ ΔButton
├────────────
│ kind = Radio
│ status = On
│ status' = Off
│ loc' = loc
│ click' = click
└────────────────────────────────────────────────────
```

2.3.5   Promotion

These mouse operations can be promoted to a full 'screen system' in a way analogous to the quad example. The various groups of radio buttons would be associated at this level.

3

Hall's Style

3.1 Notation Overview

Hall [Hall 1990] introduces some conventions for an object oriented specification style. Brownbridge [Brownbridge 1990] describes a substantial implementation project where this style was used successfully.

Hall's style adds no new features to Z; a specification written in this style uses Spivey's [Spivey 1989] notation, which gives it the advantage of a sound theoretical base. The style consists of some *conventions* for writing an object oriented specification. [Hall 1990] does propose two new schema operations, S and R, to act as a shorthand, saving the specifier a lot of writing and making the reader's task easier. These are described later.

There are five main ideas in the style that Hall describes:

- conventions for modelling object states
- use of object identities to refer to objects and express their individuality
- a convention for expressing the state of a system in terms of the objects it contains
- use of object identities to model relationships between objects
- a method of defining operations in terms of single objects and calculating their effect on the whole system, or on defined sets of objects

These techniques are explained through the examples in this section and the next. Another three aspects to the method are identified, but not covered, in Hall's paper:

- a convention for modelling classes and their relationships
- a convention for representing metaclass information
- some guidance on the meaning of inheritance and the description of subclass states and operations

Hall discusses the way in which this approach contrasts with the conventional style of specification. He also promises future support for inheritance.

3.2   Quadrilateral Example

3.2.1   Quadrilaterals and the Drawing System

Rather than describing the different kinds of quadrilaterals, we concentrate on Hall's style for defining state and operations. In describing the state we see the way in which the object oriented approach of giving each object a self property is used, and how the use of functions ensures uniqueness of the various objects.

A quadrilateral is defined using an identifier (the 'self' notion of object oriented design) as well as its other properties (defined in section 2.2).

$$
\begin{array}{|l}
\hline
\_Quad_____ \\
self : QUAD \\
edges : Edges \\
position : VECTOR \\
\hline
\end{array}
$$

The whole drawing system may be described in terms of a set of quadrilateral identifiers and a function that relates the identifier to the instance of a quadrilateral. This function ensures the individuality of the quadrilaterals. Note: we are assuming here that the drawing system deals only with quadrilaterals.

$$
\begin{array}{|l}
\hline
\_DrawingSystem_____ \\
quads : \mathbf{F}\ Quad \\
idQuad : QUAD \nrightarrow Quad \\
\hline
idQuad = \{q : quads \bullet q.self \mapsto q\} \\
\hline
\end{array}
$$

The Drawing System is thus described in terms of the objects it contains. If in turn this was part of some larger system, the whole system could be defined as a conjunction of each of the 'smaller' system schemas.

Schemas analogous to *DrawingSystem* occur frequently in this style of specification. Hall proposes an extension to the Z notation of **S**Quad as a shorthand for *DrawingSystem*.

3.2.2   Operations on Quadrilaterals

In this section we see the method for defining operations in terms of single objects and then calculating their effect on the whole system (or on defined sets of objects).

A general operation on a quadrilateral is given by

$$
\begin{array}{|l}
\hline
\_QuadOp_____ \\
\Delta Quad \\
\hline
self' = self \\
\hline
\end{array}
$$

Translation of a quadrilateral is given by

```
┌─ TranslateQuad ────────────────────────────────
│ QuadOp
│ move? : VECTOR
├────────────────────────────────────────────────
│ position' = position + move?
│ edges' = edges
└────────────────────────────────────────────────
```

The non-deterministic approach of Z could be employed here in defining a schema that changes only the *position* component. This could then be combined with other partial operation descriptions. For example

```
┌─ NewPosition ──────────────────────────────────
│ QuadOp
│ move? : VECTOR
├────────────────────────────────────────────────
│ position' = position + move?
└────────────────────────────────────────────────
```

But this describes only single objects. In order to describe the effect of the translation of one quadrilateral upon the whole drawing system the following approach is adopted

```
┌─ ChangePositionSystem ─────────────────────────
│ ΔDrawingSystem
│ q? : QUAD
│ translation? : VECTOR
├────────────────────────────────────────────────
│ idQuad' = idQuad⊕
│           {q? ↦ (μ TranslateQuad |
│                     θQuad = idQuad q? ∧ move? = translation?
│                  • θQuad')}
└────────────────────────────────────────────────
```

Careful naming is required here: *translation?* has to be used in the outer operation to avoid clashing with *move?* in the inner operation described in the included schema. As Hall points out, it is neater to decorate the included schema, thus

```
┌─ ChangePositionSystem ─────────────────────────
│ ΔDrawingSystem
│ q? : QUAD
│ move? : VECTOR
├────────────────────────────────────────────────
│ idQuad' = idQuad⊕
│           {q? ↦ (μ TranslateQuad_1 |
│                     θQuad_1 = idQuad q? ∧ move_1? = move?
│                  • θQuad_1')}
└────────────────────────────────────────────────
```

This relies upon *TranslateQuad* being deterministic. If the partial description *NewPosition* is used instead, life becomes a little more problematic.

Any operation schema generates a function from input parameters to a relation between before and after states. In this case it is described by

$$newPositionR : VECTOR \rightarrow Quad \leftrightarrow Quad$$

$$newPositionR = \{m : VECTOR \bullet$$
$$m \mapsto \{NewPosition \mid move? = m \bullet \theta Quad \mapsto \theta Quad'\}\}$$

The transformation to this form from the schema representation is automatic. However, because the types involved are different on each occasion, it cannot be defined directly in Z, and needs to be written out in full each time. Hall proposes that when a schema *Op* with inputs *INPUT* transforms a state of type *State* then $\mathbb{R}Op$ should define the corresponding function with signature $INPUT \rightarrow State \leftrightarrow State$. So $\mathbb{R}NewPosition$ would be the same as $newPositionR$.

Using the relational equivalent of functional override $\oplus_{rel}$ (Hall's definition is repeated below in section 3.2.3) the full effect of using a non-deterministic description of translation may be seen as follows:

NewPositionSystem

$\Delta DrawingSystem$
$q? : QUAD$
$move? : VECTOR$

$idQuad' \in idQuad \oplus_{rel}$
$\qquad \{NewPosition_1 \mid self = q? \wedge move_1? = move? \bullet q? \mapsto \theta Quad'\}$

3.2.3   Relational Override

First, we need to define *functions*, which maps a relation to a set of functions. Each function in the set is a subset of the relation, and has the same domain.

$=[I, X]=$

$functions : (I \leftrightarrow X) \rightarrow \mathbb{P}(I \nrightarrow X)$

$functions = \lambda r : I \leftrightarrow X \bullet \{f : I \nrightarrow X \mid dom f = dom r \wedge f \subseteq r\}$

Now we can define relational override, in which a function is overridden by a relation to give a set of functions. The individual members of the set could be obtained by overriding the function by each of the functions obtained by using *functions*.

$=[I, X]=$

$\_ \oplus_{rel} \_ : (I \nrightarrow X) \times (I \leftrightarrow X) \rightarrow \mathbb{P}(I \nrightarrow X)$

$\forall f : I \nrightarrow X; \; r : I \leftrightarrow X \bullet$
$\qquad f \oplus_{rel} r = \{g : functions \; r \bullet f \oplus g\}$

3.2.4   Creating a Quadrilateral

Here we see how uniqueness is ensured when new objects are created.

When a new quadrilateral is created its features must be set:

$$\begin{array}{|l}
\underline{\quad InitQuad}\underline{\qquad\qquad\qquad\qquad\qquad\qquad\qquad\qquad} \\
Quad \\
edges?: Edges \\
position?: VECTOR \\
\hline
edges? = edges \\
position? = position \\
\end{array}$$

We now need to describe the fact that the new quadrilateral is an object in the system with an identifier that is different from the existing ones.

$$\begin{array}{|l}
\underline{\quad CreateQuad}\underline{\qquad\qquad\qquad\qquad\qquad\qquad\qquad} \\
InitQuad \\
\Delta DrawingSystem \\
\hline
self \notin \mathrm{dom}\, idQuad \\
idQuad' = idQuad \cup \{self \mapsto \theta Quad\} \\
\end{array}$$

Let us now see what happens if creation occurs as the result of another operation, for example 'duplicate'. The duplicate operation creates a number of new quadrilaterals that are slightly overlaid so they have different positions. Each new quadrilateral is assigned an identifier and this, and the attributes provided, are fed into *InitQuad*.

$$\begin{array}{|l}
\underline{\quad Duplicate}\underline{\qquad\qquad\qquad\qquad\qquad\qquad\qquad} \\
\Delta DrawingSystem \\
shapes?: \mathbf{P}(Edges \times VECTOR) \\
\hline
\exists\, qmap: QUAD \rightarrowtail shapes? \mid \mathrm{dom}\, qmap \cap \mathrm{dom}\, idQuad = \varnothing \bullet \\
\quad idQuad' \in idQuad \oplus_{rel} \\
\quad\quad \{InitQuad \mid self \in \mathrm{dom}\, qmap \wedge (edges?, position?) = qmap\, self \bullet \\
\quad\quad\quad self \mapsto \theta Quad\} \\
\end{array}$$

Note that the new system state now includes the new quadrilaterals.

This technique of calculating the effect on the system can be extended to operations on sets of objects.

3.3   Button Example

3.3.1   Button

Hall's style recommends the object oriented approach of using a 'self' component. This approach differs from that used in the plain Z version (section 2.3). Hence the button state schema needs to be respecified. Using the same free and basic type definitions as given in the plain Z version with the additional object identifiers

[*OBJID*]

we have

$$
\begin{array}{|l}
\hline
\;\_\!\_\, Button \;\underline{\hspace{6cm}} \\
\hline
self : OBJID \\
kind : ButtonKind \\
loc : MouseLocation \\
click : MouseClick \\
action : \mathbf{P}\,ACTION \\
status : Status \\
\hline
\end{array}
$$

3.3.2   Button system

In Hall's style we identify multiple copies of the buttons using the *ButtonSystem* schema; this plays a similar rôle to the *ButtonState* schema in the plain Z version. The button system is set up as a set of buttons with unique identities using the convention for ***S****Button*, which is equivalent to the following schema

$$
\begin{array}{|l}
\hline
\;\_\!\_\, ButtonSystem \;\underline{\hspace{5cm}} \\
\hline
buttons : \mathbf{F}\,Button \\
idButton : OBJID \twoheadrightarrow Button \\
\hline
idButton = \{b : buttons \bullet b.self \mapsto b\} \\
\hline
\end{array}
$$

Creation of a new button is given by

$$
\begin{array}{|l}
\hline
\;\_\!\_\, InitButton \;\underline{\hspace{6cm}} \\
\hline
Button \\
self? : OBJID \\
kind? : ButtonKind \\
act? : Action \\
status? : Status \\
\hline
self = self? \\
kind = kind? \\
loc = Out \\
click = Up \\
(\quad kind? = Action \wedge action = act? \\
\vee \quad kind? = Toggle \wedge status = status? \\
\vee \quad kind? = Radio \wedge action = act? \wedge status = status?) \\
\hline
\end{array}
$$

When a new button is created the effect on the whole system is

$$
\begin{array}{|l}
\hline
\;\_\!\_\, CreateButton \;\underline{\hspace{5cm}} \\
\hline
InitButton \\
\Delta ButtonSystem \\
\hline
self \notin \operatorname{dom} idButton \\
idButton' = idButton \cup \{self \mapsto \theta Button\} \\
\hline
\end{array}
$$

The *CreateButton* schema ensures that when a new button is created it is given an identifier different from the identifiers of the existing buttons in the system.

The effect of encouraging the specifier always to examine the effect of an operation on the whole system is a bonus of the Hall approach. This helps to ensure that no two buttons have the same identifier.

3.3.3 Operations

In the plain Z version in section 2.3, the parts of a button that are unaffected by an operation are identified in $\Delta ButtonState$. Here similar information is given in *ButtonOp*:

```
┌─ ButtonOp ──────────────────────────────
│ ΔButton
├──────────────────────────────────────
│ self' = self
│ kind' = kind
│ action' = action
└──────────────────────────────────────
```

MouseUpButton in the plain Z version operates in a similar way to *MouseUpOp* here:

```
┌─ MouseUpOp ──────────────────────────────
│ ButtonOp
├──────────────────────────────────────
│ loc' = loc
│ click' = Up
└──────────────────────────────────────
```

3.3.4 Operations on Single Objects

Here we specify the button operations, which are described in the plain Z version, using the Hall approach. We start by looking at the details of a mouse up, as in the plain Z version this operation is described by considering the possible cases separately.

First, the mouse up can be ignored by the button, typically because it was outside the button's active area:

```
┌─ MouseUpIgnored ──────────────────────────
│ MouseUpOp
│ act! : P ACTION
├──────────────────────────────────────
│ click = Ignored
│ status' = status
│ act! = ∅
└──────────────────────────────────────
```

If the button is an action button and is primed for action, it was the recipient of the last mouse down:

┌─ *MouseUpPrimedAction* ──────────────────────────
│ *MouseUpOp*
│ *act!* : **P** *ACTION*
├──
│ *kind* = *Action*
│ *click* = *Primed*
│ *act!* = *action*
└──

If the button is a toggle button and is primed for action, then the status toggles but no action is sent out:

┌─ *MouseUpPrimedToggle* ──────────────────────────
│ *MouseUpOp*
│ *act!* : **P** *ACTION*
├──
│ *kind* = *Toggle*
│ *status'* ≠ *status*
│ *click* = *Primed*
│ *act!* = ∅
└──

If the button is a radio button and is primed for action, its status finishes up as *On* (if it was already on it stays on). If the button was *Off* then it turns on and sends a message to announce this (the purpose of the message is to tell other radio buttons in the group to turn off):

┌─ *MouseUpPrimedRadio* ───────────────────────────
│ *MouseUpOp*
│ *act!* : **P** *ACTION*
├──
│ *kind* = *Radio*
│ *click* = *Primed*
│ *status'* = *On*
│ (*status* = *Off* ∧ *act!* = *action*
│ ∨   *status* = *On* ∧ *act!* = ∅)
└──

Now the complete description for a mouse up on a button is as follows

$$MouseUp \mathrel{\widehat{=}} MouseUpIgnored$$
$$\lor\ MouseUpPrimedAction$$
$$\lor\ MouseUpPrimedToggle$$
$$\lor\ MouseUpPrimedRadio$$

The effect of a mouse up on the complete button system is given as follows

┌─ *SystemMouseUp* ────────────────────────────────
│ Δ*ButtonSystem*
│ *b?* : *OBJID*
├──
│ *idButton'* = *idButton* ⊕
│   {*b?* ↦ (μ *MouseUp* | θ*Button* = *idButton b?* • θ*Button'*)}
└──

We now look at how mouse downs and the movement of a mouse into or out of a button's active area affect the buttons. For all of these events, the status of the button does not change:

```
┌─ SameStatusOp ─────────────────────────────────
│ ΔButton
├────────────────────────────────────────────────
│ kind ∈ { Toggle, Radio } ⇒ status = status'
└────────────────────────────────────────────────
```

If there is a mouse down in the button then it becomes primed; if the mouse down is outside the mouse's active area then it is ignored

```
┌─ MouseDown ────────────────────────────────────
│ SameStatusOp
├────────────────────────────────────────────────
│ (      loc = In ∧ click = Primed
│ ∨      loc = Out ∧ click = Ignored )
│ loc' = loc
└────────────────────────────────────────────────
```

If the mouse enters or leaves a button's area then *loc* is changed

```
┌─ MouseEnter ───────────────────────────────────
│ SameStatusOp
├────────────────────────────────────────────────
│ loc' = In
│ click' = click
└────────────────────────────────────────────────
```

```
┌─ MouseLeave ───────────────────────────────────
│ SameStatusOp
├────────────────────────────────────────────────
│ loc' = Out
│ click' = click
└────────────────────────────────────────────────
```

As with the *MouseUp* operation these may be promoted quite easily to show the effect on the entire system of buttons.

In the quadrilaterals example there was some discussion of non-deterministic specification. This could be pursued here using something like

```
┌─ MouseMove ────────────────────────────────────
│ SameStatusOp
├────────────────────────────────────────────────
│ click' = click
└────────────────────────────────────────────────
```

As mentioned above, a radio button may be sent a message to tell it to turn off

$$
\begin{array}{|l}
\underline{\ TurnOff\ } \\
ButtonOp \\
\hline
kind = Radio \\
status = On \\
status' = Off \\
loc' = loc \\
click' = click \\
\end{array}
$$

3.3.5   Relationships between subsystems

In the object oriented approach objects know that they are related to other objects, but know nothing about the internal structure of the objects to which they are related. The relationship between references to objects, rather than directly between objects, means that much work is saved when items change.

We could set up a button message subsystem to manage the relationships between buttons and messages. We need the given types of button message subsystem identifiers and message identifiers

$$[BM, MESSAGE]$$

The subsystem is then defined by

$$
\begin{array}{|l}
\underline{\ ButtonMessage\ } \\
self : BM \\
bm : OBJID \nleftrightarrow MESSAGE \\
\end{array}
$$

This is an illustration of the way in which object identities are used to model relations between objects.

3.4   Conclusions

Hall's approach is a good way to give an object based style to Z specifications. However, the approach has no explicit support for class definitions or object oriented operation descriptions. It will be interesting to see the promised conventions for modelling classes and dealing with difficult issues such as inheritance.

4

Z Expression of Refinable Objects

Peter J. Whysall[1]

4.1 Introduction

This chapter describes an approach to specifying objects in Z which is particularly appropriate if the specifications are to be used for subsequent refinement and proof. When carrying out such proof it is useful to be able to provide a strong degree of separation between the objects so that it is possible to reason about the use of those objects without having to consider their internal details. The particular approach described here is motivated in some detail in [Whysall and McDermid 1991a] and [Whysall and McDermid 1991b].

Objects are described separately by so-called export and body specifications. The export specifications are algebraic in style, and describe the overall behaviour of the object independent of the internal details of the object. These export specifications can thus be used to reason about the behaviour of an object again without reference to internal details of the object. The body specifications are model oriented descriptions of the constituent parts of each object, in particular their state and methods. These body specifications are used as the basis for subsequent refinement of the objects. A proof obligation clearly exists to ensure that the export and body descriptions of an object do indeed 'say the same thing'. This issue is not discussed here but has been addressed in [Whysall and McDermid 1991b] and referred to again in the conclusions.

The remainder of this chapter briefly introduces the notation used in the specifications, and then goes on to address the quadrilateral and button examples before making a few concluding comments about the approach.

4.1.1 Export Specifications

Export specifications describe the behaviour of an object in an algebraic style based on the possible traces of the object. If the trace of an object so far is known then it is possible to determine the result of subsequent method invocations on the object. Export specifications exploit this fact, describing the result of operations

---

[1] Department of Computer Science, University of York, Heslington, York, YO1 5DD. Current address: SCE Division, Roke Manor Research Ltd., Roke Manor, Romsey, Hampshire, SO51 0ZN.

as functions of the trace so far, and additionally describing equivalences between traces.

Three special operators are introduced for representing predicates about traces, a sequencing operator for building traces, an equivalence operator between traces, and a result operator which ascribes results to traces. These operators are discussed briefly below. These operators however rely on definitions for traces and methods. Definitions for these can also be found below. These definitions are not discussed or motivated here, but are discussed in some detail in the published papers.

$$Method[Res, State] == State \rightarrow (Res \times State)$$
$$Trace[Res, State] == (Res \times State)$$

$= [R1, R2, S]$ ─────────────────────────

$(\_ ; \_) : Trace_{[R1,S]} \times Method_{[R2,S]} \rightarrow Trace_{[R2,S]}$

$\forall t : Trace_{[R1,S]};\ m : Method_{[R2,S]} \bullet$
$\quad t;\ m = m(second\ t)$

Traces are explicitly composed by applying the method to the previous trace. Note that the trace and method applied to it need not have the same result type, because the application of second throws away the result value from the existing trace.

$= [R1, R2, R3, S]$ ────────────────────

$\_ == \_ : Trace[R1, S] \leftrightarrow Trace[R2, S]$

$\forall i : Trace_{[R1,S]};\ j : Trace_{[R2,S]} \bullet$
$\quad (\forall m : Method_{[R3,S]} \bullet first(i;\ s) = first(j;\ s))$
$\quad\quad \Leftrightarrow i == j$

Two traces are equivalent if no subsequent method invocations can distinguish them. Again notice that the traces and methods need not have the same result type. (This definition is not quite as required, for it quantifies over items m of the method type, rather than real methods of the associated object. This is however the best simple definition that can be given, and illustrates the intention of the operator. More correct representations are discussed in other papers).

$= [R, S]$ ─────────────────────────────

$\_ \rightarrow \_ : Trace[R, S] \leftrightarrow R$

$\forall t : Trace_{[R,S]};\ r : R \bullet$
$\quad first\ i = r \Leftrightarrow i \rightarrow r$

The final result produced by a trace is the result of the last method applied to it.

The operators above have only been discussed extremely briefly. Hopefully a basic understanding of the purpose of each operator has been obtained, although the motivation for them will probably not be clear. A simple example of a specification using these operations is given below.

A whole export specification is represented by a single Z schema. The declarations of the schema represent the methods of the object, including any special initialization methods. The types given to these declarations uses the special method and trace types defined earlier. The predicate part of the schema describes the behaviour of the object by giving properties of the possible traces of the object. Each predicate takes one of two forms, using either the equivalence or result operator from above. If the export specification is complete, then it is possible to deduce the result of any possible method invocation on an object simply using the information in the export.

A simple stack object can be represented as shown below:

$$
\begin{array}{|l}
\underline{\;Stack\;[st]} \\
\;empty : Trace_{[elem,st]} \\
\;push : Method_{[unit,st]} \\
\;pop : Method_{[elem,st]} \\
\;isempty : Method_{[bool,st]} \\
\hline
\;\forall s : Trace_{[elem,st]};\; i : elem \bullet \\
\qquad s;\; push(i);\; pop \rightarrow i \\
\qquad s;\; push(i);\; isempty \rightarrow false \\
\qquad empty;\; pop \rightarrow error \\
\qquad empty;\; isempty \rightarrow true \\
\qquad s;\; push(i);\; pop == s \\
\qquad s;\; isempty == s
\end{array}
$$

The specification is not discussed in detail, but it is useful to make a couple of points about the predicates within it. The first part of the predicate ($s;\; push(i);\; pop \rightarrow i$) states that after any arbitrary trace, invoking the push operation followed by pop returns the value just pushed. The first equivalence in the predicate ($s;\; push(i);\; pop == s$) states that after invoking a push and pop operation after some trace the object is in a state indistinguishable from that before those two operations.

Later parts of the chapter assume a basic familiarity with the notation discussed here.

4.1.2 Body Specifications

Body specifications in this approach follow the format of standard state based specifications in Z — no special notation is introduced. The specification includes a state description schema and a collection of operation description schemas in the same way as most Z specifications do. The only difference is that within an operation schema it is now possible to refer to another object. This can be done by instantiating an earlier object, essentially by using that object's export as a type. Methods can then be invoked on the object using Z's dot notation for selection. For example a stack can be instantiated and used as follows:

$stack : Stack$
$stack.push(x)$

It is when reasoning about such use of an object that this approach is particularly valuable, for it is possible to reason about the results of these operations without expanding their body specifications.

It is not necessary to explicitly combine the parts of a body specification to form some whole, for the object is always accessed via its export which provides a single entity representing the object. It can however sometimes be useful to be able to group the parts of the body together so that they can be presented as a single whole. Under such circumstances it would be possible to utilize one of the other approaches to object oriented specification using Z to provide this description, and then to describe the behaviour of the whole using an additional export specification. This approach has been used in this way in conjunction with the Object-Z notation discussed elsewhere in this document.

4.2   Quadrilaterals

The example specifications used throughout this document are not ideally suited to this approach. In fact the objects discussed could be considered quite unusual, for they define operations which change the state of the objects, but (almost) never allow the user to invoke methods to inspect those objects. The approach to object specification described here assumes no access to an object except by its methods, and describes the behaviour of the object exactly in terms of the results of these methods. In order to describe the quadrilaterals (and subsequently buttons) it is thus necessary to include additional extractor functions on the object. Export specifications only are given for each example because, as noted above, the body specifications would be very similar to standard Z specifications. It should be appreciated therefore that the specifications below are not typical of those using this approach, but rather attempt to describe the examples used elsewhere as closely as possible.

A quadrilateral is initially null. It can be initialized with a set of vectors, and an associated position. It is possible to move and shear the quadrilateral described, essentially changing the vectors and position. Additional operations are provided to enquire of the quadrilateral what its shape and position are and whether it is indeed a quadrilateral. These correspond to seven separate methods made available on an object of the type quadrilateral.

Quad [Q]

$null : Trace_{[unit,Q]}$
$init : (\mathbf{P}\ Vector \times Vector) \rightarrow Method_{[unit,Q]}$
$quad : Method_{[bool,Q]}$
$move : Vector \rightarrow Method_{[void,Q]}$
$shear : Shear \rightarrow Method_{[void,Q]}$
$shape : Method_{[\mathbf{P}\ Vector,Q]}$
$position : Method_{[Vector,Q]}$

$\forall t : Trace_{[R,Q]};\ vs, ovs : \mathbf{P}\ Vector;\ v, pos : Vector;\ s : Shear\ |$
$\quad quad(vs) \wedge \neg (quad(ovs)) \bullet$
$\quad t;\ init(vs, pos);\ move(v) == t;\ init(vs, pos + v)$
$\quad t;\ init(vs, pos);\ shear(s) == t;\ init(s(vs), pos)$
$\quad t;\ init(vs, pos);\ position \rightarrow pos$
$\quad t;\ init(vs, pos);\ shape \rightarrow vs$
$\quad t;\ init(vs, pos);\ quad \rightarrow true$
$\quad t;\ init(ovs, pos);\ quad \rightarrow false$

The first point to note about this definition is that an explicit method to enquire whether the object is a quadrilateral has been included. This could have been avoided by making init return the appropriate truth value, essentially failing if the values were not acceptable. This would however have prevented subsequent extension to represent other objects - the init function would not have suitable for them, returning false for values which might later be deemed acceptable. This means that the object can store shapes that are not quadrilaterals. However the results of the other operations on the object are not defined in these cases, and hence an object in such a state would not be useful. Hopefully the basic behaviour described is fairly clear.

The quadrilateral specification can be expanded relatively easily to introduce other classes of geometric object. The parallelogram export can be written as follows:

Parallelogram [P]

$Quad_{[P]}$
$par : Method_{[bool,P]}$
$angle : Method_{[Angle,P]}$

$\forall t : Trace_{[R,P]};\ na, npa : \mathbf{P}\ Vector;\ pos : Vector\ |$
$\quad para(pa) \wedge \neg (para(npa)) \bullet$
$\quad t;\ init(pa, pos);\ par \rightarrow true$
$\quad t;\ init(npa, pos);\ par \rightarrow false$
$\quad t;\ init(pa, pos);\ angle \rightarrow ang(pa)$
$\quad t;\ par == t$
$\quad t;\ angle == t$

Here the definitions of the quadrilateral have been extended to include a new operation to check whether the object is a parallelogram, and another to return the angle between the edges if it is. The quad operation could also be hidden using the standard schema calculus operators if required. The other geometric objects could be produced in a similar way if required.

4.3   Buttons

The button example allows the illustration of a slightly different style of specification using this approach. Sometimes, as perhaps here, the behaviour of an object is best understood in terms of a notion of abstract state. In such circumstances having to specify long traces, while possible, can get in the way of clear specification. An approach has been devised which allows names to be given to equivalence classes over the traces. These names correspond to the abstract states which the user would perceive when interacting with the object. Equations can then be defined referring directly to these names rather than to the traces which they represent. One way to think of an object is as a state machine. In this approach the abstract states correspond directly to the states which occur in the state machine description. Additionally it is possible to parameterize the abstract states, in order to group them together, distinguishing them by the arguments passed to them.

In the case of the button system, the object can be in two main states, up and down. However these states can also be subdivided according to whether the mouse is in or out of the active region, and either primed or ignored. These are introduced as auxiliary definitions within the export specification.

$$location ::= in \mid out$$
$$Mstate ::= ignored \mid primed$$

__*Button* [B]_____

$init : Trace_{[unit,B]}$
$mouseup : Method_{[Mstate,B]}$
$mousedown : Method_{[unit,B]}$
$mouseleave : Method_{[unit,B]}$
$mouseenter : Method_{[unit,B]}$

$\forall loc : location;\ st : Mstate \bullet$
$\qquad init == up(out)$
$\qquad up(in);\ mousedown == down(in, primed)$
$\qquad up(out);\ mousedown == down(out, ignored)$
$\qquad up(out);\ mousein == up(in)$
$\qquad up(in);\ mouseout == up(out)$
$\qquad down(loc, st);\ mouseup == up(loc)$
$\qquad down(loc, st);\ mouseup \rightarrow st$
$\qquad down(in, st);\ mouseout == down(out, st)$
$\qquad down(out, st);\ mousein == down(in, st)$
$\qquad\qquad where$
$\qquad up : location \rightarrow Trace_{[R,B]}$
$\qquad down : (location \times Mstate) \rightarrow Trace_{[R,B]}$

This is not a typical example of a specification using the approach, but does illustrate the use of the notion of explicit abstract states via the named traces up and down. This issue is discussed further in [Whysall and McDermid 1991a].

4.4 Conclusions

The approach to specification of objects described in this chapter is particularly aimed at dealing with the issue of refinement. The aim is to provide a strong degree of separation between objects using the notion of exports, so that reasoning about the used objects can be done without referring to internal details of their behaviour. This is achieved by the approach, although at the expense of additional proof obligations between the export and body specifications. The additional proof obligations are however smaller, and hence the overall burden of proof remains smaller.

The benefit of the approach comes not from the specifications alone, but when trying to reason about them. The examples in this chapter therefore do not fully illustrate the approach showing only the style of specification advocated, and not the approach to reasoning. Additionally the examples required are not ideally suited to the approach, for they concentrate on considering what is going on inside an object (how its state changes), rather then how it relates to its users. Conversely, export specifications are specifically designed to describe this relationship to other objects. Nevertheless it is hoped that this chapter has illustrated the flavour of the approach, and the interested reader is referred to [Whysall and McDermid 1991a] and [Whysall and McDermid 1991b].

5

MooZ Case Studies

Silvio Lemos Meira[1]
Ana Lúcia C. Cavalcanti[2]

5.1 MooZ Notation Overview

MooZ is defined in [Meira and Cavalcanti 1991] and [Meira and Cavalcanti 1992]. The language extends Z with a number of features that provide support for object-oriented design and management of very large specifications. It is related to Object-Z, but it has a simpler semantic model.

[Meira *et al.* 1992] presents a MooZ specification of the Unix Filing System. An environment to support the construction and prototyping of MooZ specifications, ForMooZ [Meira *et al.* 1991], is under development. The aim of the project is to promote the effective use of MooZ to specify large software systems by providing an automated tool to support a software life cycle based on formal specifications.

A MooZ specification consists of a set of class definitions that can be related by some hierarchy. The general form of a class is shown in Figure 5.1. One of the classes that constitute a specification has the name of the system being defined. Its state and operations define the model that specify the system. A class name is a sequence of letters and digits that starts with an upper case letter. It is introduced at the beginning of a class definition and is repeated at the end to delimit its extent in a clear way.

5.1.1 Class Body

A class body is formed by a sequence of clauses, whose order is mandatory and whose presence is optional.

---

[1] Universidade Federal de Pernambuco, Departamento de Informática, PO Box 7851, 50.739 Recife-PE BR. E-mail: srlm@di.ufpe.br

[2] Fundação Instituto Tecnológico do Estado de Pernambuco, Grupo de Ciência e Tecnologia da Computação, PO Box 756, 50.739 Recife-PE BR. E-mail: ana@gctc.itep.br

Class $\langle$*Class-Name*$\rangle$

givensets $\langle$*type-names-list*$\rangle$

superclasses $\langle$*class-references-list*$\rangle$
$\qquad \langle$*auxiliary-definitions*$\rangle$

private $\langle$*definition-names-list*$\rangle$

or

public $\langle$*definition-names-list*$\rangle$

constants
$\langle$*axiomatic-descriptions-list*$\rangle$
$\qquad \langle$*auxiliary-definitions*$\rangle$

state
$\langle$*anonymous-schema*$\rangle$ or $\langle$*constraint*$\rangle$

initialstates
$\langle$*schema*$\rangle$
$\qquad \langle$*auxiliary-definitions*$\rangle$

operations
$\langle$*definitions*$\rangle$

EndClass $\langle$*Class-Name*$\rangle$.

Figure 5.1: General Form of a Class

givensets

The **givensets** clause introduces a list of given set names. A class whose definition includes given sets is called a generic class. A reference to such a class can instantiate (some of) them.

superclasses

MooZ allows single and multiple inheritance. The identification of the superclasses is the aim of the **superclasses** clause, which introduces a list of class references.

The definitions in the scope of a class are also in the scope of its subclasses. Name clashes among superclasses must be solved through renaming. More about inheritance is said in Section 5.1.3.

private and public

Every definition in the scope of a class (its own definitions and those of its superclasses) corresponds to a message that can be sent to an object of the class or to the class itself (see Section 5.1.6). However, this can be controlled by the **private** and **public** clauses.

The possibility of making a definition private is useful in distinguishing definitions that specify the class services from the auxiliary ones. For example, the class that represents the system model in a specification should have only the model's operations as public.

The **private** and **public** clauses apply only to the definitions introduced in the class and cannot occur simultaneously in a class definition. The **private** clause has two forms:

- **private all**
  This clause establishes that none of the definitions are visible. It is useful in classes that group auxiliary definitions only.

- **private** ⟨*definition-names-list*⟩
  The definitions whose names are listed in this clause are not visible. Any other definition can be referenced.

If a class contains more private definitions than public ones, it is more convenient to use the **public** clause in the form

public ⟨*definition-names-list*⟩

In this case, every definition is assumed to be private and only those listed in the public clause can be referenced. The form **public all** is also available for completeness and homogeneity of notation, being the default.

There are arguments in favour of using either **private** or **public** clauses. A public clause emphasizes exactly the definitions that are visible an so of interest to the clients. On the other hand, as reusability must be one of the major concerns, most of the definitions are likely to be public and so a **private** clause will be more convenient.

constants

The **constants** clause is used to introduce global constants that play an important role in the class semantics. For example, a class specifying an array can introduce two constants representing its lower and upper limits using an axiomatic description

$$n, m : \mathbb{N}$$

In this case, the specific values of n and m are not defined, so the axiomatic description contains only the declaration part.

The scope of these constants extends for the entire class body. In fact, any definition introduced in any clause is also global to the class. The **constants** clause only puts apart constants that have a special meaning in the specification, against auxiliary ones, for readability purposes.

state

The state components of a class are the ones of its superclasses and the ones introduced in its **state** clause by an anonymous schema, which is a nameless schema that can be used only to introduce state components and invariant.

For example, the anonymous schema

$$
\begin{array}{|l}
\hline
c_1 : T_1 \\
c_2 : T_2 \\
\quad\vdots \\
c_n : T_n \\
\hline
p \\
\hline
\end{array}
$$

introduces the state components c_1, c_2, ..., c_n of type T_1, T_2, ..., T_n, respectively, with p being an invariant over the state.

As the variable names in an anonymous schema represent state components, they cannot be decorated. The predicate is optional as in an ordinary schema.

The use of anonymous schemas in state definitions prevents the use of the Δ and Ξ schemas when defining operations. These schemas are a trademark of the Z style, but as the schema defining the state has no name, it cannot be referred to as a whole.

Instead, MooZ schemas defining operations can include Δ and Ξ lists. A Δ-list like

$$\Delta(c_1, c_2, \ldots, c_m)$$

corresponds to the Z schema

$$
\begin{array}{|l}
\hline
\;\Delta(c_1, c_2, \ldots, c_m) \underline{\hspace{3cm}} \\
c_1, c_1' : T_1 \\
c_2, c_2' : T_2 \\
\quad\vdots \\
c_m, c_m' : T_m \\
\hline
p \\
p' \\
\hline
\end{array}
$$

and, similarly, a Ξ-list

$$\Xi(c_1, c_2, \ldots, c_m)$$

corresponds to the Z schema

$$
\begin{array}{|l}
\hline
\,\Xi(c_1, c_2, \ldots, c_m)\, \\
\,\Delta(c_1, c_2, \ldots, c_m)\, \\
\hline
c_1 = c_1' \\
c_2 = c_2' \\
\vdots \\
c_m = c_m' \\
\hline
\end{array}
$$

This style allows the explicit declaration of the state components used in an operation definition. State components not mentioned in a Δ or Ξ-list cannot be referenced in the operation definition and it is implicitly specified that they are not modified by the operation.

Moreover, a state component declared in a Ξ-list can be referenced, but it is also the case that its value is not changed by the operation: only state components declared in a Δ-list can be modified.

Alternatively, a class can introduce only a new constraint over the state components of its superclasses. For example, suppose that a *Rectangle* class included the state components

$$
\begin{array}{|l}
\hline
height : \mathbf{R}^+ \\
width : \mathbf{R}^+ \\
\hline
\end{array}
$$

with the usual interpretation. A class *Square* defined as a subclass of *Rectangle* does not need to introduce any new state components but a constraint over the *height* and *width* values

$$\vdash height = width$$

which now characterizes a square.

initialstates

The schemas in the initialstates clause are aimed at defining the initial state of the class using initialization operations. Thus, if a schema in the initialstate clause defines an operation, the possible final states specified are the allowed initial states of the class. More than one initialization operation can be defined.

operations

The operations clause contains the schemas and semantic operations that define the class operations along with auxiliary definitions, if necessary.

5.1.2 Primitive Classes

MooZ includes primitive classes for a number of useful type constructors and mathematical definitions. They introduce in MooZ the Z Mathematical Toolkit defined in [Spivey 1989], but each type constructor is defined using a generic class and not a set and then values like partial functions or sequences are represented by MooZ objects[Meira and Cavalcanti 1992].

These classes cannot be modified. A specification can instantiate or define objects and subclasses of the primitive classes, but their definition is an intrinsic part of MooZ.

The *MathematicalDefinitions* class introduces elegant abbreviations for descriptions of type constructors and defines functions over ordinary values, sets and cartesian products. This class has the special property of being a superclass of every MooZ class except itself. The definitions introduced in *MathematicalDefinitions* are so commonly used that it is more convenient to have it as a superclass than to access the definitions through its interface.

5.1.3   Inheritance and Superclass Interfaces

Inheritance is the main reusability mechanism in object oriented languages. MooZ, in particular, has a flexible and powerful mechanism of multiple inheritance.

The superclasses clause declares the immediate superclasses of a class as a list of class references, each of which including a class name and, optionally, instantiating given sets, renaming definitions and changing visibility. Thus, the superclass interface can be conveniently adapted to the class and, as a consequence, a higher degree of reusability can be achieved.

Instantiation

Instantiation of given sets allows the reuse of generic or abstract classes when particular or more concrete versions are needed. For example, the Unix Filing System specification (from [Hayes 1987]) presented in [Meira *et al.* 1992] includes a generic class *Table* with two given sets, *ID* and *VALUE*. *Table* represents an association from *ID* to *VALUE* elements. Each subsystem of the Unix Filing System (the Storage, Channel, Naming and Access Systems) is defined as a subclass of *Table*. However, in each case *ID* and *VALUE* are instantiated as different types. The *StorageSystem* class, for example, inherits *Table* instantiating *ID* as *FID* and *VALUE* as *File*

superclasses $Table(ID \backslash FID, VALUE \backslash File)$,

where *FID* is the set of file identifiers and *File* is a class representing a file. *FID*, in particular, is also a given set, so the instantiation is done mostly for naming adequacy.

The auxiliary definitions that can be introduced in a superclasses clause are intended to define new types used to instantiate the superclasses' given sets, if necessary; however, these definitions are global to the class.

Renaming

The main purpose of renaming is to solve name clashes, but it can also be used to improve readability. If a class has more than one superclass, there can be definitions with the same name in different superclasses. If such definitions are syntactically

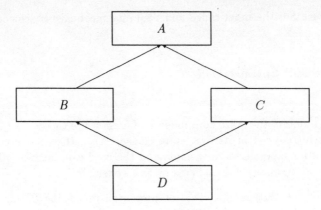

Figure 5.2: Diamond Hierarchy

equal after instantiation and renaming, then they are identified, otherwise the name clash must be solved through renaming.

A name clash can occur, for example, by inheriting from the same class in more than one way. The classical example is a diamond hierarchy such as that shown in Figure 5.2 where definitions from A are inherited by D through B and C. In this case, it is obvious that all definitions are syntactically the same, because in fact they are defined in the same class, and so are identified.

On the other hand, different superclasses with no common superclass can also have definitions with the same name. For example, classes C_1 and C_2, with no superclasses, could both have a state component c of type T. In this case, the state components would also be identified in a class D that inherits c from both C_1 and C_2.

In fact, the presence of independent definitions with the same name in C_1 and C_2, which are syntactically equal and identified in a common subclass is a strong indication that there should be a superclass common to C_1 and C_2 that extracts their commonalities. However, for cases where such commonalities do not justify the introduction of a new class, the identification of the definitions is very useful.

Repeated inheritance can also be achieved by renaming. For example, if in the diamond hierarchy (Figure 5.2) the intention is that D should include two copies of definitions from A, then they should be renamed when inherited from C or B to avoid identification.

Renaming as well as instantiation are features from Z that were promoted from the Z schemas to the class level in MooZ.

Visibility

The **private** and **public** clauses can be used to control visibility with respect to clients. However, when inheriting a class such visibility features can be changed.

A class reference in the **superclasses** clause can include **private** and **public** subclauses, which can be used to specify, respectively, that a public superclass definition is private in the subclass and, conversely, that a private superclass definition is public in the subclass. So, the inheritance and visibility mechanisms are completely independent.

5.1.4   State and Initialization

State

As mentioned before, the state components of a class are those of its superclasses and the ones introduced in its own **state** clause. Also, the class invariant is the conjunction of its superclasses invariants and the predicate introduced in its **state** clause (either in an anonymous schema or as a constraint).

For example, in the Buttons specification presented ahead, the *Button* class representing a generic button introduces two state components: *loc* is the mouse location and *click* is the state of its button. One of *Buttons'* subclasses, *OnOff*, introduces an additional state component, *status*, that represents the button state. An OnOff button is a special button that has a state which is either on or off and *OnOff* has three state components, *loc*, *click* and *status*.

Initial States

Name clashing does not affect schemas in the **initialstates** clause and the schemas with the same name in the **initialstate** of different superclasses cause no problems. If a **initialstates** clause introduces a schema named I, that will include all I schemas of its superclasses' **initialstates**.

As the state components of a class can be introduced incrementally, the aim is to define their initial values as needed, with each class defining the initial values of the state components it introduces. For example, the class *Button* mentioned above includes an schema *Init* specifying an initialization operation that defines the initial values of *loc* and *click*. *OnOff* also uses a schema named *Init* to define the initial value of *status*, defining the initial values of its state components by reusing or relying upon *Button*'s initial state definition.

Of course, when this sort of incremental definition is not adequate, the use of a schema with a different name to define the initialization operation in the subclass avoids implicit schema inclusion. Even so, schemas with the same name in different superclasses' **initialstates** do not cause name clash and the occurrences of their names in subclasses are references to their conjunction.

5.1.5   Redefinitions

Any superclass definition can be redefined in the subclass. For example, in the Drawing System example, the *Quadrilateral* class has two operations: *AngleQuad*, that rotates a quadrilateral at an angle and *ShearQuad*, that shears a quadrilateral. However, general quadrilaterals cannot be rotated, so *AngleQuad*, as defined in the *Quadrilateral* class, always yields a result indicating that the operation is not applicable.

In *Parallelogram*, a subclass of *Quadrilateral*, *AngleQuad* is redefined by another schema because a parallelogram, in particular, can be rotated. In *Rhombus*, a subclass of *Parallelogram* and, consequently, a subclass of *Quadrilateral*, the operation *ShearQuad* is redefined because it is not applicable to rhombi.

There are no type constraints and the type of the definition does not depend on the type of the corresponding one in the superclass. However, every definition accessible in the class, even those defined in the superclasses, must remain valid after the redefinition, because they are interpreted in the new context. For example, in the Buttons specification, the *Button* class defines the operation *MouseUp* that specifies the effect of releasing the mouse button:

$$MouseUp \ \hat{=}\ MouseUpButton \ \wedge \ (MouseUpIgnored \ \vee \ MouseUpPrimed)$$

MouseUpButton specifies the effect on the button state. *MouseUpIgnored* specifies that no result is produced if the mouse was being ignored by the button when it was released and, if not, *MouseUpPrimed* specifies the result.

However, the result obtained by releasing the mouse depends on the kind of button. So, *MouseUpPrimed* is redefined in the buttons subclasses *Action*, *Toggle* and *Radio* that represent particular buttons. As a consequence, *MouseUp* is indirectly redefined in these classes, because its definition refers to *MouseUpPrimed*.

Operations are likely to be redefined in order to extend or specialize a superclass operation. In the case of operations defined by schemas, extension can be easily achieved by using the schema calculus.

If a superclass definition needs to be referenced inside the subclass after being redefined, the name of the superclass can be used as a qualifier. For example, if schema S is defined in a superclass C, from the point of its redefinition onwards, S is the new definition introduced in the subclass and $S.C$ denotes the schema S as specified in C.

In fact, qualifying a definition reference using the name of the superclass where it is introduced is possible even in the absence of redefinition, but this is not necessary as there cannot be name clashes among superclasses. The exception is the schemas in the superclasses **initialstates** clause, where qualification can also be used to solve ambiguities.

Qualified messages cannot be sent to objects because a client of a class cannot use qualification to access a superclass definition. Clients cannot rely upon the hierarchic structure used to specify a class.

A renamed definition must always be accessed through its new name even when qualification is used. For example, if a superclass A contains a definition a, and its subclass B renames a to b, then a qualified reference to a must be $b.A$ and not $a.A$.

5.1.6   Objects and Messages

Every object is an instance of a class that has a state and may answer to messages as specified in the class. In MooZ, an object is a record whose fields represent the state specified in its class, with each field corresponding to a state component. The field is named after the state component and its value has the type of the state component.

Thus, a MooZ class specifies the common features of its objects. The state component names, types and the state invariant are defined in a class. An object, on the other hand, is a value. Each state component of an object has a particular value satisfying the state invariant.

Object Messages

Objects communicate by sending messages, with notation $o\ m$ used to represent the fact that message m is sent to object o. Here is where the syntax for the common Z structures deviate from the standard.

A class also specifies the messages its objects can answer to, which are called object messages. These are all the state components, all the schema defining operations, which may be identified by the presence of Δ and Ξ-lists, and the semantic operations.

The answer to a state component message is its value. The answer to a schema message is the schema definition itself. As schemas can be manipulated using the schema calculus, the possibility of getting a schema as result of a message is very useful.

However, a schema definition may refer to definitions in the class scope but that are not directly in the client scope. For example, in the Drawing System specification, the *Quadrilateral* class has the state components defined in the following anonymous schema:

$$
\begin{array}{|l}
\hline
v1, v2, v3, v4 : Vector \\
position : Vector \\
\hline
\ldots \\
\hline
\end{array}
$$

$v1$, $v2$, $v3$ and $v4$ represent the quadrilateral edges and *position*, its position. Moreover, *Vector* is a given set. *MoveQuad*, the operation that moves a quadrilateral, is defined by

$$
\begin{array}{|l}
\hline
\_MoveQuad_____ \\
\Delta(position) \\
move? : Vector \\
\hline
position' = position + move? \\
\hline
\end{array}
$$

The *DrawingSystem* class is a *Quadrilateral* client. Its definition involves the declaration of a quadrilateral object q to which *MoveQuad* can be sent.

As *MoveQuad* refers to definitions that are not in the *DrawingSystem* scope (such as *position* and *Vector*), the actual answer to this message has to access these definitions through the q and *Quadrilateral* interfaces.

The *MoveQuad* extension in *Quadrilateral* is

```
┌─ MoveQuad ────────────────────────────────────────────────
│ Δ(position, v1, v2, v3, v4)
│ move? : Vector
├────────────────────
│ position' = position + move?
│ v1' = v1
│ v2' = v2
│ v3' = v3
│ v4' = v4
└────────────────────────────────────────────────────────────
```

Thus the answer to the message *q MoveQuad* is

```
┌─ MoveQuad ────────────────────────────────────────────────
│ Δ(q)
│ move? : Quadrilateral Vector
├────────────────────
│ q' position = q position (Quadrilateral+) move?
│ q' v1 = q v1
│ q' v2 = q v2
│ q' v3 = q v3
│ q' v4 = q v4
└────────────────────────────────────────────────────────────
```

There is no problem if some definition in the schema text is private and, as so, not accessible by a client. In fact, a private definition cannot be directly accessed by a client because it is not available as a message, but can be accessed through other public definitions.

Class Messages

Some definitions, namely given sets, schema and free types, abbreviations and constants defined by axiomatic descriptions are not available from objects. Instead, they correspond to class messages because they are state independent.

The notation used for a class message is similar to that for objects. For a class C and a message m, $C\ m$ represents the sending of a message m to C.

The answer to a given set, schema, free type or abbreviation message is the type specified by the corresponding definition. Such result can be used to define more complex types using the MooZ type constructors. The answer to a constant message is a value of the constant type, including objects and functions, that satisfies its specification.

Class messages allow access to state independent definitions even when no object of the class is available.

This short introduction sums up the basic features of MooZ. We now give the specification of the Drawing System and Buttons.

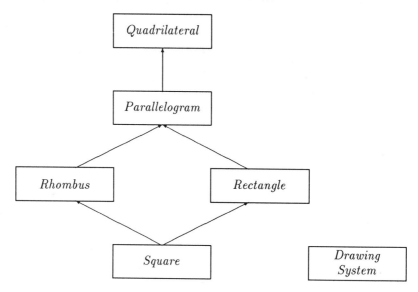

Figure 5.3: Drawing System Specification Hierarchy

5.2 Drawing System

A Drawing System groups different sorts of quadrilaterals associated to identifiers. The quadrilaterals considered are general quadrilaterals themselves, parallelograms, rhombi, rectangles and squares. Figure 5.3 shows the hierarchic structure used in the specification.

The *Quadrilateral* class represents a general four-sided figure and the subclasses (*Parallelogram*, *Rhombus*, *Rectangle* and *Square*) particular sorts of quadrilaterals as their names suggest. The *DrawingSystem* class specifies the system itself.

Class *Quadrilateral*

The definition of a quadrilateral uses vectors and scalars. Moreover, some quadrilaterals can be sheared and a shearing factor is used for that end. As these entities do not need a model in this specification, they are represented by given sets.

givensets *Vector, Scalar, Shear*

The operations on vectors are the usual ones and can be introduced by an axiomatic description.

constants

$$
\begin{array}{l}
\_ + \_: Vector \times Vector \rightarrow Vector \\
| \_ |: Vector \rightarrow Vector \\
\_ . \_: Vector \times Vector \rightarrow Scalar \\
0 : Vector
\end{array}
$$

A quadrilateral can be specified by its edges, four vectors, and for the Drawing System its position is also important. Therefore, the state is

state

$v1, v2, v3, v4 : Vector$
$position : Vector$

$v1 + v2 + v3 + v4 = 0$

The invariant states that the sum of the vectors representing the edges is zero.

operations

The operation for moving a quadrilateral is easily defined by

---
MoveQuad _____

$\Delta(position)$
$move? : Vector$

$position' = position + move?$

The operation that shears a quadrilateral is specified here, but it will be redefined in the sequel to establish that it is not applicable to squares, rhombi and rectangles.

ShearQuad _____

$s? : Shear$

Definitions omitted

Rotation is not defined for a general quadrilateral; its specification is also given here because it is highly desirable to have the operation available for the whole range of quadrilaterals, although it only returns an error message in this case.

AngleQuad _____

$r! : MESSAGE$

$r! = OperationNotApplicable$

MESSAGE is a free type with just one constant representing an error message.

$MESSAGE \; :: \; OperationNotApplicable$

EndClass *Quadrilateral*.

Class *Parallelogram*

Parallelograms are special kinds of quadrilaterals,

superclasses *Quadrilateral*

and every operation in *Quadrilateral* is inherited. However, *AngleQuad* is well defined for a parallelogram and must be redefined. For this purpose, we introduce the type *Angle* via a given set and some usual operations on it.

givensets *Angle*

constants

$$
\begin{array}{|l}
cos^{-1} : Scalar \nrightarrow Angle \\
\_/\_ : Scalar \times Scalar \nrightarrow Scalar
\end{array}
$$

The property that characterizes a parallelogram is defined as an additional property over the state components inherited from *Quadrilateral*;

state

$$
\vdash v1 + v3 = 0
$$

operations

and the new definition for *AngleQuad* is

$$
\begin{array}{|l}
\underline{\quad AngleQuad \quad}\\
\Xi(v1, v2) \\
a! : Angle \\
\hline
a! = cos^{-1}((v1.v2)/(\mid v1 \parallel v2 \mid))
\end{array}
$$

EndClass *Parallelogram*.

Note that the form of definition just used above is typical of simple object oriented specifications: parallelograms are quadrilaterals whose opposite sides are parallel and equal in length and for which rotation – and consequently *AngleQuad* – is well defined.

It is of course a case of single inheritance, but it already shows some advantages of the object oriented approach when compared to the plain Z specification, since the latter needs to be initially cluttered with details which in our case will appear naturally, in place, and only when needed.

Class *Rhombus*

A rhombus is a parallelogram,

superclasses *Parallelogram*

with the additional property

state

$$\vdash\; \mid v1 \mid = \mid v2 \mid$$

operations

and for which the operation *ShearQuad* is not defined. So, it is redefined here to return an error message.

```
┌─ ShearQuad ─────────────────────────────────
│  r! : MESSAGE
│ ─────────────────
│  r! = OperationNotApplicable
└──────────────────────────────────────────────
```

This definition is quite straightforward

EndClass *Rhombus*.

and the definition of a rectangle is quite similar:

Class *Rectangle*

superclasses *Parallelogram*

state

$$\vdash\; v1.v2 = 0$$

operations

```
┌─ ShearQuad ─────────────────────────────────
│  r! : MESSAGE
│ ─────────────────
│  r! = OperationNotApplicable
└──────────────────────────────────────────────
```

EndClass *Rectangle*.

Defining a square is even simpler, given that it is a rhombus and a rectangle, simultaneously.

Class *Square*

Using multiple inheritance, we write

superclasses *Rhombus, Rectangle*

and it is done.

EndClass *Square*.

The Drawing System associates identifiers to a set of quadrilaterals,

Class *DrawingSystem*

with the set of quadrilateral identifiers represented by the type

givensets *QID*

and the state being a mapping from *QID* to *Quadrilateral*.

state

$$
screen : Map(X \backslash QID, Y \backslash Quadrilateral)
$$

initialstates

$$
\begin{array}{l}
\underline{Init} \\
\Delta(screen) \\
screen'\ Init
\end{array}
$$

In the initial state, the *DrawingSystem* does not contain any quadrilateral. The state component *screen* is in its initial state which is defined via a schema also named *Init* in its class, *Map*, a primitive class representing the standard map type constructor.

operations

The drawing system has the usual operations for adding and removing quadrilaterals.

$$
\begin{array}{l}
\underline{AddQuad} \\
\Delta(screen) \\
q? : Quadrilateral \\
\hline
\exists\, qid : QID \mid qid \notin screen\ dom \bullet screen' = screen \oplus \{qid \mapsto q?\}
\end{array}
$$

$$
\begin{array}{l}
\rule{6cm}{0.4pt}\\
\_\,DeleteQuad\,\rule{5cm}{0pt}\\
\Delta(screen)\\
qid? : QID\\
\rule{3cm}{0.4pt}\\
qid? \in screen\ dom\\
screen' = screen \vartriangleleft \{qid?\}\\
\rule{6cm}{0.4pt}
\end{array}
$$

dom, $\oplus$ and $\vartriangleleft$ are operations defined in the class *Map* with the usual meaning.

There are three operations for updating a quadrilateral, *MoveQuad*, *AngleQuad* and *ShearQuad*. These operations need to be applied to a particular quadrilateral in the Drawing System. Initially a framing schema for operations that update a quadrilateral is specified.

$$
\begin{array}{l}
\_\,UpdateDrawingSystem\,\rule{4cm}{0pt}\\
\Delta(screen)\\
qid? : QID\\
q, q' : Quadrilateral\\
\rule{5cm}{0.4pt}\\
qid? \in screen\ dom\\
q = screen\ qid?\\
screen' = screen \oplus \{qid? \mapsto q'\}
\end{array}
$$

MoveDS, that moves a quadrilateral, can be defined using *UpdateDrawingSystem* and *MoveQuad*. Moreover, as q and q' are auxiliary variables, they must be hidden in the final definition.

$$
MoveDS \;\hat{=}\; (\,UpdateDrawingSystem \wedge_q MoveQuad\,)\backslash(q, q')
$$

The definitions for *AngleDS* and *ShearDS* are similar and omitted here.

EndClass *DrawingSystem*.

5.3 Buttons

This example specifies different kinds of screen buttons. Figure 5.4 shows the class hierarchy used in this specification. *Button* is an abstract class (it has no instances) that represents a generic button and its subclasses represent some special kinds of buttons.

Class *Button*

A number of schemas in this class are auxiliary and thus private.

private *MouseUpButton, MouseUpIgnored, MouseUpPrimed*

Some buttons perform actions when clicked. These actions are represented here by the type *ACTION*, which is introduced as a given set.

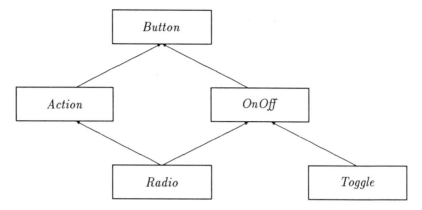

Figure 5.4: Buttons Specification Hierarchy

givensets *ACTION*

A button is sensitive to the location of the mouse and to the movement of the mouse button.

state

$loc : MouseLocation$
$click : MouseClick$

The mouse can be located either in or out of the button's active area.

$MouseLocation \; :: \; In \mid Out$

The mouse button can be either released (up) or depressed, in which case the button can be either primed for action or the mouse is being ignored.

$MouseClick \; :: \; Up \mid Primed \mid Ignored$

In the initial state, the mouse is outside the button and the mouse button is released.

initialstates

Init _____
$\Delta(loc, click)$

$loc' = Out$
$click' = Up$

---

operations

The button performs operations that correspond to mouse actions. The mouse can either enter or leave the button's active area.

```
┌─ MouseEnter ────────────────────────────────
│ Δ(loc)
├─────────────
│ loc' = In
└─────────────────────────────────────────────
```

```
┌─ MouseLeave ────────────────────────────────
│ Δ(loc)
├─────────────
│ loc' = Out
└─────────────────────────────────────────────
```

The mouse button can be clicked: in this case, if the mouse is in the button's active area, the mouse becomes primed, otherwise the mouse is ignored.

```
┌─ MouseDown ─────────────────────────────────
│ Δ(click)
│ Ξ(loc)
├─────────────
│ loc = In ∧ click' = Primed ∨
│ loc = Out ∧ click' = Ignored
└─────────────────────────────────────────────
```

The mouse button can be released. In this case, the mouse click state changes to *Up*.

```
┌─ MouseUpButton ─────────────────────────────
│ Δ(click)
├─────────────
│ click' = Up
└─────────────────────────────────────────────
```

In response to the click, the button performs a set of actions. If the mouse was being ignored before the click, no action is performed and so this set is empty.

```
┌─ MouseUpIgnored ────────────────────────────
│ Δ(click)
│ act! : P ACTION
├─────────────
│ click = Ignored
│ act! = ∅
└─────────────────────────────────────────────
```

If the mouse was primed, the set of actions depends on the kind of button. Therefore, this set will not be specified in this generic class.

```
┌─ MouseUpPrimed ─────────────────────────────
│ Δ(click)
│ act! : P ACTION
├─────────────
│ click = Primed
└─────────────────────────────────────────────
```

The *MouseUp* operation is then defined as

$$MouseUp \,\hat{=}\, MouseUpButton \land (MouseUpIgnored \lor MouseUpPrimed)$$

EndClass *Button*.

Now we turn to the specification of action buttons.

Class *Action*

superclasses *Button*

An action button performs some actions when selected. These actions are represented here by a constant whose value is the set of actions that can be performed by the button.

constants

$$\mid \quad action : \mathbf{P}\, ACTION$$

The *MouseUpPrimed* operation on buttons must be extended to specify that the resulting set of actions, *act!*, is equal to *action*.

operations

$$MouseUpPrimed \,\hat{=}\, MouseUpPrimed \mid act! = action$$

In MooZ, schema definitions are inherited without expansion. So, *MouseUp*, whose definition depends on *MouseUpPrimed*, is also specialized for an action button as a consequence of redefining *MouseUpPrimed*.

EndClass *Action*.

Class *OnOff*

This is also an abstract class representing buttons whose status can be either on or off.

superclasses *Button*

state

$$\boxed{\; status : Status \;}$$

$$Status \;::\; On \mid Off$$

Its initial state is defined as an operation that receives the initial status as input.

initialstates

```
 ___ Init _____
| Δ(status)
| status? : Status
|_____
| status' = status?
|
|_____
```

As the schema defining the initial state in *Button* is also named *Init*, it is implicitly included in the above one. *OnOff*'s initial state is actually defined by the resulting schema.

EndClass *OnOff*.

Class *Toggle*

A toggle button is an OnOff button that toggles its state when selected. So, it inherits from *OnOff*

superclasses *OnOff*

operations

with the single difference that the *MouseUpPrimed* operation must be extended to establish that no action is performed and the status toggles.

```
 ___ MouseUpPrimed _____
| MouseUpPrimed
| Δ(status)
|_____
| status' ≠ status
| act! = ∅
|_____
```

EndClass *Toggle*.

Radio buttons present another case of multiple inheritance given that

Class *Radio*

a radio button is an action and OnOff button at the same time. A renaming is needed because *Action* redefines *MouseUpPrimed*, generating a name clash.

superclasses *Action*, *OnOff*[*MouseUpPrimed\MouseUpPrimedOnOff*]

operations

A radio button is switched on when selected; if it was switched off before, it executes the set of actions, otherwise nothing happens.

$$
\begin{array}{|l}
\_\textit{MouseUpPrimed}_____ \\
\textit{MouseUpPrimedOnOff} \\
\Delta(\textit{status}) \\
\hline
(\textit{status} = \textit{Off} \wedge \textit{act!} = \textit{action} \vee \\
\textit{status} = \textit{On} \wedge \textit{act!} = \varnothing) \\
\textit{status'} = \textit{On}
\end{array}
$$

A radio button is associated with a group of other radio buttons. If some radio button in a group is switched on, the others are asked to turn off.

$$
\begin{array}{|l}
\_\textit{TurnOff}_____ \\
\Delta(\textit{status}) \\
\hline
\textit{status} = \textit{On} \\
\textit{status'} = \textit{Off}
\end{array}
$$

EndClass *Radio.*

Acknowledgements

The research reported here is supported by The Brazilian Science Research Council – CNPq – and The Pernambuco State Science Foundation – FACEPE. The authors would like to thank Augusto Sampaio (PRG, Oxford) for his patient help with the originals.

6

Object-Z

Gordon Rose[1]

6.1 Object-Z Overview

6.1.1 Introduction

Object-Z [Carrington *et al.* 1990], [Duke and Duke 1990], [Duke *et al.* 1991] is an extension of the formal specification language Z [Hayes 1987], [Spivey 1989], [Woodcock and Loomes 1988] to accommodate object orientation [Meyer 1988], [Booch 1991]. The main reason for this extension is to improve the clarity of large specifications through enhanced structuring.

A Z specification typically defines a number of state and operation schemas. A state schema groups together variables and defines the relationship that holds between their values. At any instant, these variables define the state of that part of the system which they model. An operation schema defines the relationship between the 'before' and 'after' states corresponding to one or more state schemas. Therefore, inferring which operation schemas may affect a particular state schema requires examining the signatures of all operation schemas. In large specifications this is impracticable. Conventions, such as chapters, group states and operations informally, but cannot enforce structure.

Object-Z overcomes this problem by confining individual operations to refer to one state schema. The definition of a state schema with the definitions of its associated operations (and those of other components to be detailed later) constitute a *class*.

A class is a template for *objects* of that class: for each such object, its states are instances of the class' state schema and its individual state transitions conform to individual operations of the class. An object is said to be an instance of a class and to evolve according to the definitions of its class.

A class may specify part of a system, so that the potential behaviour of that part may be considered and understood in isolation. Complex classes can be specified to inherit other classes, or to include references to objects. These structuring mechanisms are called *inheritance* and *instantiation* respectively.

---

[1] Software Verification Research Centre, Department of Computer Science, University of Queensland, Queensland 4072, Australia.

An Object-Z specification of a system typically includes a number of class definitions related by inheritance and instantiation which build towards a class representing the entire system.

Section 6.1.2 introduces the syntax of classes and outlines some semantic issues. Section 6.1.3 demonstrates instantiation and Section 6.1.4 inheritance. Section 6.2 illustrates the application of Object-Z to the Quadrilaterals Example and Section 6.3 to the Buttons Example.

6.1.2   Classes

Class Definition

Syntactically, a class definition is a named box, optionally with generic parameters. In this box the constituents of the class are defined and related. Possible constituents are: a visibility list, inherited classes, type and constant definitions, a state schema, an initial state schema, operation schemas, and a history invariant.

```
┌─ ClassName[generic parameters] ──────────────────────
│  visibility list
│  inherited classes
│  type definitions
│  constant definitions
│  state schema
│  initial state schema
│  operation schemas
│  history invariant
│
└───────────────────────────────────────────────────────
```

The visibility list, if included, restricts access to the listed features (feature is defined below) of objects of the class. If omitted, all features are visible. Visibility is not inherited so that a derived class may nominate any inherited feature as visible.

Inheritance is described in Section 6.1.4, and type and constant definitions are as in Z.

The state schema is nameless and comprises declarations of state variables and a state predicate. Constants and state variables are collectively called *attributes*. The conjunction of any predicate imposed on the constants and the state predicate is called the *class invariant*.

The attributes and class invariant are implicitly included in the initial state schema and each operation schema. In addition, the state variables and predicate in primed form are implicitly included in the operation schemas. Hence the class invariant holds at all times: in each possible initial state and before and after each operation.

The initial state schema is distinguished by the keyword *INIT*: in conjunction with the implicit class invariant, it defines the possible initial states (i.e. initialization is not restricted to a unique state).

Operation schemas differ from Z operation schemas in that they have a Δ-list of those individual state variables whose values may change when the operation is applied to an object of the class (this is in contrast to the granularity of the Δ convention in Z which applies to entire schemas).

Attributes and operations are collectively called *features*.

The *history invariant* is a predicate over histories of objects of the class (typically in temporal logic) which further constrains the possible behaviours of such objects.

A generic stack example

Consider the following specification of the generic class *Stack*. We adopt the Z style of writing explanatory text on detail after the formal specification.

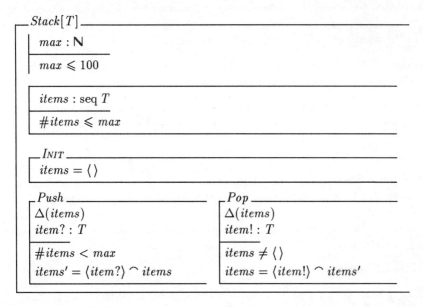

The class has a constant *max* which does not exceed 100. Distinct *Stack* objects may have different values of *max*, each remaining constant throughout the evolution of the particular stack.

The state schema has one state variable *items* denoting a sequence of elements of the generic type T. The state invariant stipulates that the size of the sequence cannot exceed *max*. An initialized stack has no items.

Operation *Push* prepends a given input *item?* to the existing sequence of items provided the stack has not already reached its maximum size.

The understanding of a Δ-list is that state variables not listed are unchanged. In *Push* then, *items* is subject to change, and the second conjunct of *Push* specifies the change (without that conjunct, *items* would become unspecified).

Operation *Push* implicitly expands to:

$$
\begin{array}{|l}
\hline
\ \_Push \_\rule{5cm}{0.4pt} \\
\quad max : \mathbb{N} \\
\quad items, items' : \mathrm{seq}\ T \\
\quad item? : T \\
\hline
\quad max \leqslant 100 \\
\quad \#items \leqslant max \\
\quad \#items' \leqslant max \\
\quad \#items < max \\
\quad items' = \langle item? \rangle \frown items \\
\hline
\end{array}
$$

By convention, no Δ-list is equivalent to an empty Δ-list. When operations are compounded to define new operations, the Δ-list of the result is the merge of the individual Δ-lists. In the expansion of a compound operation, only state variables not in the resultant Δ-list are implicitly unchanged.

Operation *Pop* outputs a value *item!* defined as the head of sequence *items* and reduces *items* to the tail of its original value.

When a class is applied, actual types replace generic types, and features and operation parameters may be renamed as, for example, in the following class descriptor:

$$Stack[\mathsf{N}][nats/items, nat?/item?, nat!/item!]$$

The scope of renaming is the whole class, except that variables of a particular operation may be renamed by qualifying the substitution by the operation's name, e.g. $Push[nat?/item?]$. Simultaneous substitution is indicated by list pairs as in '$(x, y/y, x)$'. Care must be taken when renaming to avoid conflicts with existing bound variables.

Outline of Semantics

Following is an informal description of some aspects of Object-Z semantics.

Declaration $c : C$ declares c to be a reference to an object of the class described by C.

There is no implication that an object reference declaration introduces a distinct object reference and by implication a distinct object, nor does the declaration imply that the introduced object is initialized. Thus, declaration $c, d : C$ need not mean that c and d reference distinct objects. If the intention is that they do so at all times, then the predicate $c \neq d$ would be included in the class invariant. If c and d are to refer to distinct objects initially, but subsequently are to refer synonymously to the same object, then $c \neq d$ would be a predicate of *INIT* but an operation would, for example, specify $c' = d$ (with c in the operation's Δ-list).

The term $c.att$ denotes the value of attribute *att* of the object referenced by c, and $c.Op$ denotes the evolution of that object according to the definition of C's Op.

The semantics of an Object-Z class is similar to the semantics of a Z system with one state schema: it comprises a set of attribute bindings consistent with the attribute signatures and class invariant, a set of initial bindings, and a set of relations on attribute bindings, each relation corresponding to an operation with specific parameters. A history or trace semantic model includes the sequences of possible bindings and corresponding relations, further constrained by any history invariant.

The advantage of adopting object references is that the object referenced by c may evolve without changing the value of c. This is particularly significant in modelling aggregates as it effectively eliminates the need for 'framing' which is often used when modelling aggregates in Z. For example, the declaration $sc : \mathsf{F}\, C$ can model an aggregate of objects which may evolve without changing the value of sc, as the object references do not change. Evolution of a constituent object is effected by defining a selection environment such as:

$$
\begin{array}{|l}
\_\text{Select}\rule{6cm}{0.4pt} \\
\ c? : C \\
\hline
\ c? \in sc \\
\end{array}
$$

and applying it as in:

$$Op \mathrel{\widehat{=}} Select \bullet c?.Op$$

This effectively 'promotes' the operation Op on the selected object to be an operation on the aggregate, which in this example happens to be also named Op. (The notation $schema_1 \bullet schema_2$ means that variables declared in the signature of $schema_1$ are accessible when interpreting $schema_2$. That is, the scope of $schema_1$ is extended to the end of $schema_2$'s text. The resulting schema is semantically identical to the conjunction of $schema_1$ and $schema_2$.)

Several objects of the aggregate may undergo an evolutionary step concurrently using a multiple selection environment such as:

$$
\begin{array}{|l}
\_\text{SelectTwo}\rule{6cm}{0.4pt} \\
\ c_1?, c_2? : C \\
\hline
\ c_1? \neq c_2? \\
\ \{c_1?, c_2?\} \subseteq sc \\
\end{array}
$$

and applying it as in:

$$TwoStep \mathrel{\widehat{=}} SelectTwo \bullet (c_1?.Op_1 \wedge c_2?.Op_2)$$

Distributed operation conjunction may be used to specify an operation in which all aggregated objects are subject to the same operation Op concurrently, e.g

$$AllStep \mathrel{\widehat{=}} \textstyle\bigwedge c : cs \bullet c.Op$$

With reference semantics, an object reference, such as c or d above, is only Δ-listed if the reference may change value and refer to another object. A set variable, such as sc above, is only Δ-listed if the set may change value, i.e. if references are added, removed or substituted.

6.1.3 Instantiation

Objects may have object references as attributes, i.e. conceptually, an object may have constituent objects. Such references may either be individually named or occur in aggregates: the two cases are illustrated in this section.

Two Stacks Example

Consider the class *StackPair* which contains two individually named references to stacks of natural numbers.

$$NatStack == Stack[\mathbb{N}][nats/items, nat?/item?, nat!/item!]$$

```
┌─ StackPair ──────────────────────────────────────────
│  ┌──────────────────────────────────────────────────
│  │ s₁, s₂ : NatStack
│  │ s₁ ≠ s₂
│  ├──────────────────────────────────────────────────
│  │ #s₁.nats ⩽ #s₂.nats
│  ├──────────────────────────────────────────────────
│  │ ┌─ INIT ──────────────────────────────────────────
│  │ │ s₁.INIT ∧ s₂.INIT
│  │ └──────────────────────────────────────────────────
│  │ Push₁ ≙ s₁.Push
│  │ Push₂ ≙ s₂.Push
│  │ PushBoth ≙ Push₁ ∧ Push₂
│  │ PushOne ≙ Push₁ [] Push₂
│  │ [other operations]
└──────────────────────────────────────────────────────
```

$StackPair$ class:

$s_1, s_2 : NatStack$

$s_1 \neq s_2$

$\#s_1.nats \leqslant \#s_2.nats$

$INIT$: $s_1.INIT \wedge s_2.INIT$

$Push_1 \mathrel{\widehat{=}} s_1.Push$

$Push_2 \mathrel{\widehat{=}} s_2.Push$

$PushBoth \mathrel{\widehat{=}} Push_1 \wedge Push_2$

$PushOne \mathrel{\widehat{=}} Push_1 \;[]\; Push_2$

$[other\ operations]$

It is intended that the references s_1 and s_2 do not change, so they are declared as constants. Moreover, it is intended that the referenced stacks be distinct, hence the references are explicitly distinguished. The state invariant requires that the size of the first stack does not exceed that of the second.

Operation $Push_1$ promotes s_1's *Push* operation to be an operation of *StackPair*. Its implied expansion is:

$Push_1$ schema:

$s_1, s_2 : NatStack$

$s_1.max : \mathbb{N}$

$s_1.nats, s_1.nats' : \text{seq}\,\mathbb{N}$

$nat? : \mathbb{N}$

$s_1 \neq s_2$

$\#s_1.nats \leqslant \#s_2.nats$

$\#s_1.nats' \leqslant \#s_2.nats'$

$s_1.max \leqslant 100$

$\#s_1.nats \leqslant s_1.max$

$\#s_1.nats' \leqslant s_1.max$

$\#s_1.nats < s_1.max$

$s_1.nats' = \langle nat? \rangle \frown s_1.nats$

As s_1 and s_2 are declared to be constants, neither s_1' nor s_2' appear in the expansion, i.e. s_1 and s_2 continue to refer to their respective objects. The primed form of the state invariant follows from the interpretation that $(s_1.nats)'$ is $s_1'.nats'$ which is $s_1.nats'$ as s_1 is constant. The interpretation of $s_1.nats'$ is the value of the *nats* attribute of the object referenced by s_1 after $Push_1$.

Operation *PushBoth* is the conjunction of the above expansion with a similar expansion with qualification by 's_2.' instead of 's_1.' The individual push operations proceed independently except that the same value *nat?* applies to both.

Operation *PushOne* is a compound operation involving choice. The choice operator '[]' indicates nondeterministic choice of one operation from those constituent operations with satisfied preconditions. Thus, the choice is deterministic if exactly one precondition is satisfied and the construct fails if no precondition is satisfied. The interfaces of the several operations must be identical.

Stack Aggregation Example

As a second example of instantiation, consider an aggregation of a fixed but arbitrary number of stacks. We wish to push an item onto, or pop an item from, any stack in the aggregation, and to transfer an item from one stack to another.

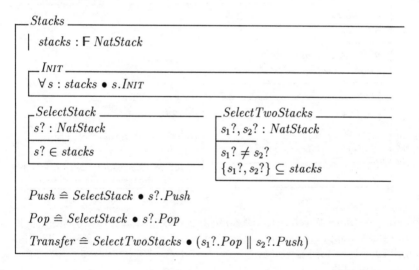

The parallel operator, '$\|$', used in the definition of *Transfer* above, achieves inter-object communication. The operator conjoins operation schemas but also identifies (equates) and hides inputs and outputs having the same type and basename (i.e. apart from '?' or '!'). The parallel operator is not associative – input/output equating and hiding apply to the conjunction (which is associative).

6.1.4   Inheritance

Inheritance is a mechanism for incremental specification, whereby new classes may be derived from one or more existing classes. Inheritance therefore is particularly significant in the effective reuse of existing specifications.

The type and constant definitions of the inherited classes and those declared explicitly in the derived class are merged. Similarly, the schemas of the inherited classes and those declared explicitly in the derived class are merged. Any schemas with the same name (or in the case of state schemas, without a name) are conjoined. The history invariants of the inherited classes and that of the derived class are also conjoined.

Name clashes, which lead to unintentional merging, can be resolved by renaming when nominating inherited classes.

Indexed Stack Example

We can derive an indexed stack from *Stack* by adding a distinguished stack position.

$$
\begin{array}{l}
\rule{0pt}{1em}\text{\underline{\textit{IndexedStack}[T]}}\\
\textit{Stack}[T]\\
\hline
\begin{array}{l}
\textit{index} : \mathbb{N}_1\\
\hline
\textit{items} \neq \langle\,\rangle \Rightarrow \textit{index} \in \text{dom}\,\textit{items}
\end{array}\\[1em]
\begin{array}{l}
\text{\underline{\textit{SetIndex}}}\\
\Delta(\textit{index})\\
n? : \mathbb{N}_1\\
\hline
n? \in \text{dom}\,\textit{items}\\
\textit{index}' = n?
\end{array}\\[1em]
\begin{array}{ll}
\text{\underline{\textit{Push}}} & \text{\underline{\textit{Pop}}}\\
\Delta(\textit{index}) & \Delta(\textit{index})\\
\hline
\textit{items} \neq \langle\,\rangle \Rightarrow & \textit{index} = 1 \wedge \textit{items}' \neq \langle\,\rangle \Rightarrow\\
\quad \textit{index}' = \textit{index} + 1 & \quad \textit{index}' = 1\\
 & \textit{index} \neq 1 \Rightarrow \textit{index}' = \textit{index} - 1
\end{array}
\end{array}
$$

The index continues to relate to the same item except that if the top item is indexed and the stack popped, the index then relates to the new top item. The index is unspecified if the stack is empty.

6.2   Quadrilaterals Example

It is assumed that readers are familiar with the context of this example from its Z specification early in the book.

$$[Scalar, Angle]$$
$$Vector == Scalar \times Scalar$$

$|\_|$: $Vector \rightarrow Scalar$
$\_+\_$: $Vector \times Vector \rightarrow Vector$
$\_.\_$: $Vector \times Vector \rightarrow Scalar$
$rotate$: $Vector \times Angle \rightarrow Vector$
$\mathbf{0}$: $Vector$

[*definitions omitted*]

─── *QuadFig* ─────────────────────────

v_1, v_2, v_3, v_4 : $Vector$

$v_1 + v_2 + v_3 + v_4 = \mathbf{0}$

──*Angle*──────────────────────
angle! : $Angle$

QuadFig captures the notion of a quadrilateral figure with no notion of position. *Angle* is introduced, but its definition is deferred.

─── *Quad* ─────────────────────────
QuadFig

$position$: $Vector$

──*Move*──────────────────────
$\Delta(position)$
$vec?$: $Vector$

$position' = position + vec?$

──*Shear*──────────────────────
[*definition omitted*]

A *Quad* is a *QuadFig* with a distinguished position. Movement via *Move* is relative to the current position. A *Quad* may be sheared but detail is omitted. *Angle* is inherited but not further defined.

─── *Parallelogram* ─────────────────────
Quad

$v_1 + v_3 = \mathbf{0}$

──*Angle*──────────────────────
angle! : $Angle$

$angle! = cos^{-1}(v_1 \, . \, v_2 \, / \, |v_1| \, |v_2|)$

Parallelogram's definition of *Angle* is merged with the inherited definition.

Rhombus

Parallelogram

$|v_1| = |v_2|$

$Shear \triangleq [false]$

Rhombus's definition of Shear is merged with the inherited definition thereby rendering it inapplicable.

Rectangle

Parallelogram

$v_1 \cdot v_2 = 0$

$Shear \triangleq [false]$

Square

Rhombus
Rectangle

DrawingSystem

$screen : \mathsf{F} \downarrow Quad$

AddQuad

$\Delta(screen)$
$quad? : \downarrow Quad$

$quad? \notin screen$
$screen' = screen \cup \{quad?\}$

DeleteQuad

$\Delta(screen)$
$quad? : \downarrow Quad$

$quad? \in screen$
$screen' = screen \setminus \{quad?\}$

SelectQuad

$quad? : \downarrow Quad$

$quad? \in screen$

$Move \triangleq SelectQuad \bullet quad?.Move$
$Angle \triangleq SelectQuad \bullet quad?.Angle$
$Shear \triangleq SelectQuad \bullet quad?.Shear$

State variable *screen* is a finite set of references to ↓*Quad* (i.e. to a *Quad* or any of its derivatives). Object reference semantics eliminates the need for explicit quadrilateral identifiers, and a set (in contrast to a function) suffices for aggregation. Also, no 'framing' schema is required. Polymorphism is achieved with the drawing system's operations as a given value of *quad?* satisfying *SelectQuad* identifies the particular class derived from *Quad*.

6.3   Buttons Example

6.3.1   Introduction

A screen-based console consists of various kinds of button arranged in clusters. Instead of having physical buttons, each button is represented by an icon on the screen. A button is selected by moving a mouse-driven cursor into the button's icon region and depressing the mouse button (the mouse has only one button). The selected console button is said to be 'primed'. On subsequently releasing the depressed mouse button, even if the mouse has moved, the primed console button is activated and is no longer primed. At any time, at most one console button is primed.

If the mouse button is depressed while the cursor is not within any icon region, no button is primed, and consequently on release, no button is activated. The mouse can be moved to any screen location.

Once a button has been primed, the priming cannot be cancelled, i.e. activation can only be delayed (by delaying the release of the mouse button). Normally, the operator would simply click (down then up) the mouse button while over the selected icon.

There are three kinds of button:

(i) An *action* button has an associated constant sequence of actions which is output when the button is activated. Different action buttons may output different (but constant) action sequences. An action button does not have a state — it simply outputs its action sequence. Actions are not further specified: it is assumed that action sequences are enacted elsewhere in the system.

(ii) A *toggle* button may be *on* or *off*. On activation, it changes its state (toggles) and, for uniformity as will be seen, outputs the empty action sequence.

(iii) A *radio* button is also either *on* or *off*, but on being activated to *on* also outputs a sequence of actions in the same way as an action button. Radio buttons are always in a cluster and at any time exactly one of the buttons is *on*. On activating another radio button in the cluster, the previous on button is automatically switched off. If the on button is reselected it outputs the empty sequence of actions.

The console has one cluster of action buttons, one cluster of toggle buttons and one cluster of radio buttons.

At this level of abstraction, button icon shapes and locations are not detailed, nor are there any restrictions on cluster or action-sequence size. The specification does not provide for introducing or removing buttons or for relocating or reshaping button icons.

The specification proceeds by first describing an inheritance hierarchy which includes the action-, toggle- and radio-button classes. Next, clusters of each of these three kinds of button are specified, and the three clusters are collected together to model the total set of buttons. Then a primer and locator are specified to facilitate priming and button referencing (via location) respectively. Next, the mouse is described, and finally the console is modelled.

In the descriptions below, detailed explanatory text is placed after the referenced formal text.

6.3.2   The Button Hierarchy

```
┌─ Button ──────────────────────────────────────────────
│ ┌────────────────────────────────────────────────────
│ │
│ └────────────────────────────────────────────────────
└───────────────────────────────────────────────────────
```

Button is a virtual class which exists only to provide a common ancestor for all kinds of button.

```
┌─ BinaryButton ────────────────────────────────────────
│ Button
│ ┌────────────────────────────────────────────────────
│ │ on : Boolean
│ ├────────────────────────────────────────────────────
│ │ ┌─ INIT ─────────────────────────────────────────
│ │ │ ¬ on
│ │ └─────────────────────────────────────────────────
│ └────────────────────────────────────────────────────
└───────────────────────────────────────────────────────
```

A *BinaryButton* has two states. At this stage of derivation, no provision is made for changing the state.

```
┌─ OnOffButton ─────────────────────────────────────────
│ BinaryButton
│ ┌─ On ─────────────────────     ┌─ Off ──────────────
│ │ Δ(on)                         │ Δ(on)
│ ├───────────────────────         ├─────────────────────
│ │ ¬ on ∧ on'                    │ on ∧ ¬ on'
│ └───────────────────────         └─────────────────────
└───────────────────────────────────────────────────────
```

An *OnOffButton* is derived from *BinaryButton* and provides for changing the state via explicit turn on and turn off operations.

```
┌─ ToggleButton₀ ───────────────────────────────────────
│ BinaryButton
│ ┌─ Toggle ──────────────────────────────────────────
│ │ Δ(on)
│ ├────────────────────────────────────────────────────
│ │ on' = ¬ on
│ └─────────────────────────────────────────────────────
└───────────────────────────────────────────────────────
```

ToggleButton$_0$ is also derived from *BinaryButton* and provides for changing the state by defining *Toggle*.

[*Action*]

Action denotes the set of all actions.

```
┌─ActionButton──────────────────────────────────────
│ ↾(Activate)
│ Button
│ │  actions : seq Action
│ ┌─Activate──────────────────────────────────────
│ │ acts! : seq Action
│ ├──────────────────────────────────────────────
│ │ acts! = actions
└─┴──────────────────────────────────────────────
```

An *ActionButton* is derived directly from *Button*. Being stateless, initialization is not applicable. It has an associated constant sequence of actions, and operation *Activate* outputs the sequence. On instantiation, individual action buttons may have different action sequences. The ↾-list indicates visibility, i.e. the list of features accessible via the interface. For this case study, visibility lists are included only in classes which are subsequently instantiated.

```
┌─ToggleButton──────────────────────────────────────
│ ↾(INIT, Activate)
│ ToggleButton₀[Activate/Toggle]
│ ActionButton
├──────────────────────────────────────────────────
│ │  actions = ⟨ ⟩
└─┴────────────────────────────────────────────────
```

ToggleButton extends the conventional toggle button *ToggleButton$_0$*. Renaming *Toggle* to *Activate* merges that operation with the inherited *ActionButton*'s *Activate*. The resulting *Activate* combines the toggle action with the output of an action sequence, in this case constrained to be empty.

```
┌─RadioButton───────────────────────────────────────
│ ↾(on, Activate, Off)
│ OnOffButton[Activate/On]
│ ActionButton
└───────────────────────────────────────────────────
```

A *RadioButton* has the traits of both an *OnOffButton* and an *ActionButton*. The radio button must output its action sequence on being set to on. This is achieved by renaming *On* to *Activate* which merges the switching role with the inherited *ActionButton*'s *Activate*.

6.3.3   Clusters of Buttons

Having defined action, toggle and radio buttons, classes representing clusters of
each kind are now defined. The definitions use the set as the clustering device.

$$
\begin{array}{|l}
\hline
\underline{\ ActionButtons\ } \\
\restriction(buts, Activate) \\
\hline
\quad buts : \mathsf{F}\ ActionButton \\
\hline
\quad \begin{array}{|l}
\underline{\ Select\ } \\
\quad but? : \downarrow Button \\
\hline
\quad but? \in buts \\
\hline
\end{array} \\
\hline
\quad Activate \;\hat{=}\; Select \bullet but?.Activate \\
\hline
\end{array}
$$

Select ensures that the given button *but?* is a member of the set *buts* and by
implication is an *ActionButton*. However, *but?* is typed as a reference to $\downarrow Button$,
i.e. to a *Button* or any of its derivatives; this widens the applicability of the cluster
as will be seen later. On activation, the selected action button outputs its action
sequence. Set *buts* is specified as a constant because the specification does not
require buttons to be removed, added or substituted.

$$
\begin{array}{|l}
\hline
\underline{\ ToggleButtons\ } \\
\restriction(buts, \textsc{Init}, Activate) \\
\hline
\quad buts : \mathsf{F}\ ToggleButton \\
\hline
\quad \begin{array}{|l}
\underline{\ \textsc{Init}\ } \\
\quad \forall\, but : buts \bullet but.\textsc{Init} \\
\hline
\end{array} \\
\hline
\quad \begin{array}{|l}
\underline{\ Select\ } \\
\quad but? : \downarrow Button \\
\hline
\quad but? \in buts \\
\hline
\end{array} \\
\hline
\quad Activate \;\hat{=}\; Select \bullet but?.Activate \\
\hline
\end{array}
$$

ToggleButtons is identical in structure to *ActionButtons* except that initialization
is included. On activation, the selected button is toggled and outputs the empty
action sequence.

```
┌─ RadioButtons ──────────────────────────────────────────────
│ ↾(buts, Activate)
│
│ │ buts : F RadioButton
│
│ ┌──────────────────────────────────────────────────────────
│ │ on_but : RadioButton
│ ├──────────────────────────────────────────────────────────
│ │ on_but ∈ buts
│ │ on_but.on
│ │ ∀ but : buts \ {on_but} • ¬ but.on
│ └──────────────────────────────────────────────────────────
│ ┌─ SelectNew ──────┐ ┌─ ReSelect ──────┐ ┌─ EmptyActs ──────┐
│ │ Δ(on_but)        │ │ but? : ↓Button  │ │ acts! : seq Action│
│ │ but? : ↓Button   │ ├─────────────────┤ ├───────────────────┤
│ ├──────────────────┤ │ but? = on_but   │ │ acts! = ⟨ ⟩       │
│ │ but? ∈ buts      │ └─────────────────┘ └───────────────────┘
│ │ but? ≠ on_but    │
│ │ on_but' = but?   │
│ └──────────────────┘
│
│ Activate ≙ (SelectNew • but?.Activate ∧ on_but.Off)
│             []
│             ReSelect ∧ EmptyActs
└──────────────────────────────────────────────────────────────
```

RadioButtons is more complex because at all times exactly one button must be on. The class invariant requires that *on_but* identifies the on button, and that the remaining buttons are off. This invariant precludes every *RadioButton* from being initialized. The choice of initial on button is nondeterministic. Operation *SelectNew* succeeds when a new radio button (*but?*) in the cluster is selected: it changes *on_but* to the new button. When a new button is selected, the cluster's *Activate* operation changes *on_but* and outputs the action sequence corresponding to the new on button. If the same button is reselected, operation *ReSelect* is enabled and *Activate* simply outputs the empty action sequence via *EmptyActs*. The [] operator chooses whichever is enabled — the preconditions are disjoint.

6.3.4   The Totality of Buttons

```
┌─ Buttons ──────────────────────────────────────────────────
│ ↾(buts, INIT, Activate)
│
│ │ act_buts : ActionButtons
│ │ tog_buts : ToggleButtons
│ │ rad_buts : RadioButtons
│ │ buts : F ↓Button
│ ├──────────────────────────────────────────────────────────
│ │ let buts_list == ⟨act_buts.buts, tog_buts.buts, rad_buts.buts⟩ •
│ │     buts_list partitions buts
│
│ ┌─ INIT ──────────────────────────────────────────────────
│ │ tog_buts.INIT
│ └──────────────────────────────────────────────────────────
│
│ Activate ≙ act_buts.Activate [] tog_buts.Activate [] rad_buts.Activate
└──────────────────────────────────────────────────────────────
```

Class *Buttons* assembles the three button clusters: it requires that the corresponding three sets of buttons be disjoint and collectively constitute *buts*. This is achieved by the 'partitions' class invariant. The operation *Activate* chooses exactly one of the three cluster operations, provided the given *but?* is in *buts*; if not, the operation fails. In order for *Activate* to have a well-defined interface, the signatures of the three alternatives must be identical — they are, namely: *but?* : ↓*Button*; *acts!* : seq *Action*.

Assuming *Activate* succeeds, then regardless of which button is selected, an action sequence (possibly empty) is output.

6.3.5   The Primer

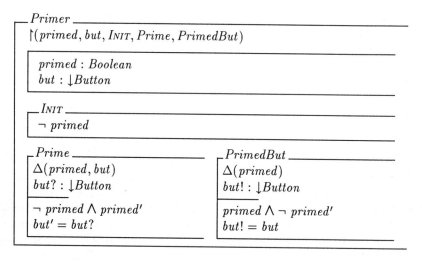

Class *Primer* retains priming information: if *primed*, *but* is the primed button. Operation *Prime* sets the primer and records the selected button. The *PrimedBut* operation outputs the primed button and clears the primer. By defining *but* of type *Button* or derivative, the primer is applicable to each of the three kinds of button.

6.3.6   The Locator

[*Location*]

Location denotes the set of all locations on the screen.

```
┌─ Locator ─────────────────────────────────────────────────────
│ ↾(buts, ButAtLoc, LocOut)
│ ┌──────────────────────────────────────
│ │ but_at_loc : Location ↠ ↓Button
│ │ buts : F ↓Button
│ ├──────────────────────────────────────
│ │ buts = ran but_at_loc
│ │ ┌─ ButAtLoc ──────────────    ┌─ LocOut ────────────────
│ │ │ loc? : Location              │ loc? : Location
│ │ │ but! : ↓Button               ├────────────────────────
│ │ ├──────────────────────        │ loc? ∉ dom but_at_loc
│ │ │ loc? ∈ dom but_at_loc
│ │ │ but! = but_at_loc(loc?)
```

Class *Locator* is concerned with the relationship between button location and button identification. A partial function, *but_at_loc* denotes the relationship: the set of locations corresponding to a button in its range represents the icon region occupied by that button. The locator accommodates any mix of the three kinds of button.

Given any location within some button's icon region, *ButAtLoc* returns the button's reference. *LocOut* detects locations not within any button's icon region. The specification omits means for introducing, removing or relocating buttons, or for changing icon shapes.

6.3.7 The Mouse

```
┌─ Mouse ──────────────────────────────────────────────────
│ ↾(INIT, Move, DownLoc, Up)
│ ┌──────────────────────────
│ │ down : Boolean
│ │ loc : Location
│ ├── INIT ──────────────────
│ │ ¬ down
│ │ ┌─ Down ──────────        ┌─ Up ──────────
│ │ │ Δ(down)                  │ Δ(down)
│ │ ├─────────────             ├───────────────
│ │ │ ¬ down ∧ down'           │ down ∧ ¬ down'
│ │ ┌─ Move ──────────        ┌─ Loc ──────────
│ │ │ Δ(loc)                   │ loc! : Location
│ │ │ loc? : Location          ├───────────────
│ │ ├─────────────             │ loc! = loc
│ │ │ loc' = loc?
│ │ DownLoc ≙ Down ∧ Loc
```

Class *Mouse* has two state variables, namely an up-down Boolean indicator and a location. Operation *DownLoc* corresponds to depressing the mouse button and outputting the current location.

6.3.8 The Console

```
┌─ Console ──────────────────────────────────────────────────
│ ↾(INIT, Move, Prime, MisPrime, Activate, Ignore)
│ ┌────────────────────────────────────────────────────
│ │ buttons : Buttons
│ │ primer : Primer
│ │ locator : Locator
│ │ mouse : Mouse
│ ├────────────────────────────────────────────────────
│ │ locator.buts = buttons.buts
│ ├────────────────────────────────────────────────────
│ │ primer.primed ⇒ primer.but ∈ buttons.buts
│ ├────────────────────────────────────────────────────
│ │ ┌─ INIT ──────────────────────────────────────────
│ │ │ buttons.INIT ∧ primer.INIT ∧ mouse.INIT
│ ├────────────────────────────────────────────────────
│ │ Move ≙ mouse.Move
│ │ Prime ≙ mouse.DownLoc ‖ locator.ButAtLoc ‖ primer.Prime
│ │ MisPrime ≙ mouse.DownLoc ‖ locator.LocOut
│ │ Activate ≙ mouse.Up ∧ (primer.PrimedBut ‖ buttons.Activate)
│ │ Ignore ≙ mouse.Up ∧ [¬ primer.primed]
└─────────────────────────────────────────────────────────────
```

The final class, *Console*, assembles the buttons, the primer, the locator and the mouse. The class invariant requires that the primed button, if any, is one of the console's buttons, and that the locator is concerned specifically with this console's buttons.

Operation *Move* simply promotes mouse movement to console level.

Prime succeeds if the mouse's button is depressed while the cursor is located over some button icon. The locator translates the location output by the mouse to a button which is retained by the primer. The parallel operator hides both the location and button parameters.

MisPrime succeeds if the mouse's button is depressed while the cursor is not located over any button icon. The location parameter is hidden.

Thus, on depressing the mouse's button, either *Prime* or *MisPrime* occurs.

On releasing the mouse's button (regardless of location), if a button is primed it is activated (operation *Activate*), otherwise the release is ignored (operation *Ignore*).

Externally, the console requires an operator to move the mouse and depress and release its button. The console outputs an action sequence (possibly empty) on each successful activation.

Acknowledgements

The financial support of AOTC (Australia) and contributions to the development of Object-Z by Cecily Bailes, David Carrington, David Duke, Roger Duke, Ian Hayes, Paul King, Anthony Lee and Graeme Smith are gratefully acknowledged.

7

OOZE

Antonio J. Alencar and Joseph A. Goguen[1]

7.1 An Overview of OOZE

OOZE, which stands for 'Object Oriented Z Environment', is intended for both the early and the late specification phases of the system life cycle, and includes facilities for rapid prototyping. OOZE uses the graphical notation and comment conventions of Z, formalizes its style, and adapts it to fit the object oriented paradigm, allowing declarations for *classes*, *attributes* and *methods* within modules. Attributes can be class-valued, that is, *complex objects* are supported. Modules can be generic, are organized hierarchically, and help with structuring and reusing specifications and code. Modules can be linked by views, which assert relationships of refinement. Both the syntax and semantics of module interfaces can be specified precisely by using theories.

In OOZE, *objects* (which are instances) are carefully distinguished from *class declarations* (which serve as templates for objects). Objects are also organized into *meta-classes*, for ease of identification and to support iteration. Multiple inheritance is supported for both classes and modules. Overloading and exception handling are also supported. All of this has a precise semantics that is based upon order sorted, hidden sorted algebra. Also, OOZE has an interpretable sublanguage that can be used for rapid prototyping, and a compilable sublanguage that can be used for implementation. By providing animation facilities for rapid prototyping, OOZE helps to improve communication with the client, and makes it easier to master its mathematical basis.

Ultimately, OOZE is a programming environment designed to take advantage of the attractive properties of formal methods while reducing the burden associated with their use. This environment includes not just a syntax checker, type checker, and an interpreter for an executable sublanguage, but also a theorem prover and a module database; all of this is based on facilities provided by the OBJ3 system [Goguen *et al.* 1992b] and 2OBJ [Goguen *et al.* 1992a]. OOZE can also help with subsequent phases of system development, including design, coding and maintenance. As a result, OOZE should reduce the time and cost of formal methods, and also increase confidence in correctness.

---

[1] Oxford University Computing Laboratory, Programming Research Group, 8–11 Keble Road, Oxford, OX1 3QD.

Some readers may question what is the justification for a language inspired by Z that is neither a proper extension of Z nor based upon set theory, but rather upon algebra. The reasons for choosing to modify Z rather than just extend it are several: First, we believe that some of the very nice stylistic conventions of Z should be more than mere conventions — they should be enforced. For example, we wish to prohibit introducing new constraints on old data and operations at arbitrary points in a specification; such freedom allows radical violations of encapsulation, and is also contrary to the principles of object orientation, and indeed of good specification in any paradigm. Moreover, we think it is important to provide proper modules, with generic capability. Finally, the scope conventions for declarations in Z are unnecessarily complex, partly due to the excessive mobility of schemas; this is reflected in the complexities of the semantics given by Spivey [Spivey 1988].

OOZE looks and acts like a model-based language, and indeed, it provides the same meaning for common set theoretic constructions, such as product and power, as well as for lists, partial functions, total functions, and all the operations upon these that are familiar from Z. Thus, the models of OOZE specifications are equivalent to models of corresponding Z specifications, when these exist. However, the underlying semantic formalism used to define these models is different: OOZE uses algebra, whereas Z uses a Zermello-Frankel-like set theory based on axioms given in first order logic (an elementary introduction to Zermello-Fraenkel axiomatic set theory can be found, for example, in [Enderton 1977]).

Unfortunately, it can be very difficult to reason about complex set theoretic constructions founded on axioms in first order logic. Reasoning about algebraic specifications can be significantly simpler, and it can also be easier to support mechanical verification in this approach; indeed, it was relatively easy to implement OOZE precisely because of this, based on facilities provided by OBJ. A more complete introduction to OOZE can be found in [Alencar and Goguen 1991].

7.1.1   Modules

By convention, a Z schema with non-decorated variables represents the state space of some system component, and is followed by another schema defining the initial values for those variables, and by other schemas defining operations on these variables. But these conventions are not enforced, and it is very easy to write specifications that violate them. Indeed, new relationships among variables can be added anywhere.

OOZE groups the state space schema, initial state schema, and operation schemas into a single unit called a *module*. (This structure was inspired by that of Object-Z [Duke *et al.* 1991].) Only the operations defined in this unit are allowed to act upon the objects of that class. Syntactically, such a unit is an open-sided named box in which the features of the class are defined, with the following general form,

```
┌─Class class-name < ancestor-names──────────────────────────────
│
│  constants
│   ┌─State───────────────────────────────────────────────────
│   │ class attributes
│   │ ─────────────
│   │ class invariant
│   └──────────────────────────────────────────────────────────
│   ┌─Init────────────────────────────────────────────────────
│   │ initial values
│   └──────────────────────────────────────────────────────────
│
│  methods
│
└────────────────────────────────────────────────────────────────
```

where **class-name** is the name of the class and the symbol $<$ indicates that the
class being defined is a subclass of one or more previously defined classes, named
in **ancestor-names**. The **constants** are fixed values which cannot be changed by any
method, and are the same for all instances of the class. The **class attributes** are
variables that can take values either in another class or in a data type. The **class
invariant** is a predicate that constrains the values that the attributes can take; it
must hold for all objects of the class, before and after the execution of methods
and in the initial state. *Init* gives the **initial values** that attributes take. **methods** are
given in schemas that define operations involving one or more attributes of the same
class, and possibly input or output variables; these define the relationship between
the state of an object before and after the execution of a method. (Differences
between the syntax of schemas in OOZE and Z are discussed in Section 7.1.4).

7.1.2   Encapsulation of Classes in Modules

In many object oriented languages, including Eiffel [Meyer 1992], Smalltalk [Gold-
berg and Robson 1983] and Object-Z [Duke *et al.* 1991], modules and classes are
identified, so that only one class can be encapsulated. Because of this, cases where
several classes have interdependent representations are not easily captured. For
example, consider a class **Private-Teachers** and a class **Independent-Students**,
where each class has only one attribute, with a value involving the other class:
teachers keep a list of their students, and students keep a list of their teachers.
Because these two classes are interdependent, it is impossible to determine which
should be defined first. If no order is established, then the object hierarchy is not
properly enforced. A straightforward solution is to introduce both classes in one
module. Hence OOZE modules can contain any number of classes, and can also
be generic:

```
┌─ module-name[parameters] ─────────────────────────────────────────
│
│  ┌─ Importing ────────────────────────────────────────────────────
│  │ imported − modules
│  │
│  ┌─ Class class-name₀ ────────────────────────────────────────────
│  │   ⋮
│  │
│
│      ⋮
│
│  ┌─ Class class-nameₙ ────────────────────────────────────────────
│  │   ⋮
│  │
│
└────────────────────────────────────────────────────────────────────
```

Here **module-name** names the module; **parameters** is a list of formal names with their corresponding requirements on the actual parameters that instantiate the module; **imported-modules** lists the imported modules, and **class-name**$_0, \dots,$ **class-name**$_n$ are the classes defined in the module. Note the clear distinction between module importation and class inheritance. The former has to do with the scope of declarations; for example, a class cannot be used unless the module that declares it is imported. Note that module importation is *transitive*, so that if A imports B and B imports C, then everything in C is also available in A. See [Goguen 1984] and [Goguen 1991] for more detailed discussions of the module concepts used in OOZE, including importation and genericity; they are evolved from those introduced in Clear [Burstall and Goguen 1980] and implemented in OBJ [Goguen *et al.* 1992b], and are given a precise semantics using concepts from category theory.

7.1.3 Parameters and Theories

It can be very useful to define precisely the properties that the actual parameters to a parameterized module must satisfy in order for it to work correctly; in OOZE these properties are given in a *theory*; theories are a second kind of module in OOZE. In particular, theories can be parameterized and can use and inherit other modules. The main syntactic difference between theories and other modules is that axioms in theories can be arbitrary first order sentences, whereas other modules are more limited in order to ensure executability. A theory is introduced in an open-sided box, with its name preceded by the key word *Theory*.

Theories declare properties and provide a convenient way to document module interfaces. Understandability, correctness, and reusability are improved by this feature. Also, theories provide loose specifications of data and objects, and in conjunction with views they can be used to assert invariants for objects of a given class. Semantically, a theory denotes the variety of order sorted, hidden sorted algebras that satisfies it. If no new classes are introduced in a theory, then the variety of order sorted algebras satisfying it is its semantics. See [Alencar and Goguen 1991] for further discussion of the semantics of theories. For example, the following theory requires that an actual parameter provide a totally ordered set with a given element:

Theory TotalOrder

$[X]$

v: X

$\quad \_ \sqsubset \_ : X \leftrightarrow X$

$\forall x, y, z : X \bullet$
$\quad \neg(x \sqsubset x)$
$\quad (x \sqsubset y) \wedge (y \sqsubset z) \Rightarrow (x \sqsubset z)$
$\quad (x \sqsubset y) \vee (x = y) \vee (y \sqsubset x)$

Here the notation $[X]$ indicates that X is a set newly introduced for this specification.

The formal parameters of an OOZE module are given after its name in a list, along with the requirements that they must satisfy. The actual parameters of generic modules are not sets, constants and functions, but rather modules. The motivation for this is that the items that naturally occur in modules are usually closely related, so that it is natural to consider them together rather than separately. Moreover, by allowing parameters to be modules, OOZE incorporates the powerful mechanisms of parameterized programming [Goguen 1984]. In the syntax below, $P_0, P_1, \cdots, P_n$ are the formal module names, while $T_0, T_1, \cdots, T_n$ are theory names:

---
module-name$[P_0 :: T_0, P_1 :: T_1, \cdots, P_n :: T_n]$

$\vdots$

$\vdots$

7.1.4   Method Schemas

In both OOZE and Z, schemas are used to define key aspects of systems. However in OOZE executable and loose specifications are clearly distinguished — theories are used for loose specifications of objects (see Section 7.1.3 for an overview of the use of theories) and modules other than theories are used for executable specifications. Although schemas are used in both kinds of specifications to describe methods that act upon objects, the predicate part of an executable module schema differs from that of a non-executable one, and from a Z schema. While in loose specification schemas and Z schemas the values of variables before and after method application are related by arbitrary first order sentences, in executable module schemas a more restricted form is used, in which those values are related by conditional equations. Non-executable specification schemas have the following general form:

---
schema_name

declarations

---

first order sentence

---

first order sentence

$\vdots$

Here, the conjunction of all sentences is taken as the first order sentence that relates the values of variables when a method is used. Executable module schemas have the following general form:

```
┌─schema_name──────────────────────────────────────────────
│ declarations
│ ─────────────
│ equations
│   if predicate
│ ─────────────
│ equations
│   if predicate
│
│ ⋮
└──────────────────────────────────────────────────────────
```

Here, the *if* clause can be considered a pre-condition, and the respective equations are required to hold if the condition, expressed by a predicate, is *true*. If the *if* clause is omitted, then the equations must hold in any circumstance.

In both loose and executable specifications, the value of an attribute before method application is indicated by an undashed variable, while the dashed (') variables indicate the value after. Method inputs are indicated by variables with an interrogation mark (?), and outputs by variables with an exclamation mark (!). Also, **declarations** may contain a list of attributes whose values can be changed by the method. This list is headed by Δ, and attributes absent from it do not change (this feature was inspired by Object-Z [Duke *et al.* 1991]), that is, the dashed attribute value equals the undashed one. The absence of a Δ list means that no attribute value can be changed by the method. (*Init* is an exception to this rule; its signature has no Δ list, and only dashed variables are available. The anomalous nature of *Init* is due to the fact that it is really a method of the meta-class, rather than the class.) Unlike Z, these are not mere conventions; they are part of the definition of OOZE, and they are enforced by the implementation.

7.1.5   Applying Methods

In OOZE, the following syntax indicates that a certain method acts on a certain object,

object.method($p_0, p_1, \cdots, p_n$)

where **object** is an object name, **method** is a method name for the class to which **object** belongs, and $p_0, p_1, \cdots, p_n$ are parameters whose types must agree with those of the corresponding formal parameters. Actual parameters are associated with formal parameters according to the order in which the latter are declared. The method *Init* is an exception, because it acts on no objects, and its syntax is simplified to the form $Init(p_0, p_1, \cdots, p_n)$.

Also, OOZE provides a selection function for each visible attribute of a class, indicated by a dot before the attribute name. So if A is an object of a class that has b as an attribute, then $A.b$ yields the current value of that attribute in A.

7.1.6   Meta-Classes

Meta-classes are a powerful concept that makes reasoning and specifying simpler, by allowing specifications that are easier to create, understand and update. The basic idea is to associate to each class of objects a meta-class that provides access to its instances.

In OOZE, every object has a unique identifier that is set when it is created, and a specification of a class X defines a meta-class $\overline{X}$. $\overline{X}$ has only one instance, with identifier $\overline{X}$, and one visible attribute, called *objs*, that contains a list of all the objects of class X. Note that every time an object is created, its identifier is added to the list kept by its meta-class, as well as to the meta-classes of its ancestors. These meta-classes allow us to define methods that act upon all or part of the objects of a class, by using the built-in meta-class method Map having the general form

meta_object. Map(objects, f)

where meta_object is the unique instance of a meta-class, objects is a list (or alternatively a set) of objects upon which the operation f is required to act (it may be a method or a function).

Often the meta-object can be inferred by the parser from the operation f, and in any case, it can be inferred from the class name, so that we could always write $X \bullet Map(objs, f)$ for $\overline{X} \bullet Map(objs, f)$, and usually write just $Map(objs, f)$, or even $Map(f)$.

7.2   Quadrilaterals

Let us consider a system in which squares, rectangles, rhombi, parallelograms and general quadrilaterals can be created, modified and deleted. An initial attempt to specify this system in an object-oriented discipline would possibly consider using a class hierarchy where *Quadrilateral* is the most general class, *Parallelogram* is a subclass of *Quadrilateral, Rhombus* and *Rectangle* are both subclasses of *Parallelogram*, and *Square* is concurrently a subclass of Rhombus and Rectangle.

At first sight that hierarchy seems appropriate because quadrilaterals are general four-sided closed geometric figures, parallelograms are quadrilaterals that have parallel opposite sides, rhombi are parallelograms with sides of equal length, rectangles are parallelograms with perpendicular sides, and squares are geometric figures that are both rectangles and rhombi. Nevertheless, one may wonder if this hierarchy is still a reasonable design option if geometric figures are allowed to be sheared. Note that the result of shearing rhombi, rectangles and squares cannot be guaranteed to yield geometric figures of those respective kinds.

It may be tempting to try to get a class hierarchy that strictly represents the one initially proposed by making a method *Shear* available for quadrilaterals, and either making it hidden or undefined in the specification of rhombus and rectangle. However this would produce a specification unsafe from the dynamic binding point of view. A future reuse of the same specification could lead to the existence of input variables, output variables, and attributes that take value in the *Quadrilateral* class and that may dynamically point to a figure in which an operation defined in its ancestor is undefined in that specific descendent. Another solution is to make shearing free of effects in *Rhombus*, *Rectangle* and *Square*, that is, such that it does not change the object upon which it acts. A third possible solution is to specify *Shear* as a method of the *Quadrilateral* class that yields a new quadrilateral, redefine it in the *Parallelogram* class to yield a new parallelogram, and let it be inherited unaltered by the other classes.

While the first solution makes reuse more difficult the second one makes an operation available in an environment in which it should not be. Moreover the third solution, although elegant, produces new objects when this may be undesirable. A solution which avoids all these problems is to create a *ShearableQuadrilateral* class and a *ShearableParallelogram* class; this approach has been taken in the executable OOZE specification that follows.

The theory *Vector* that follows specifies the requirements that a formal parameter to the module *Quadrilaterals* should satisfy.

Theory Vector _____

$[VECTOR, SCALAR]$

$\_ + \_ : VECTOR \times VECTOR \to VECTOR$
$|\_| : VECTOR \to SCALAR$
$\_ \cdot \_ : VECTOR \times VECTOR \to SCALAR$

(definitions omitted)

$[ANGLE]$

$cos^{-1} : SCALAR \to ANGLE$
$\_/\_ : SCALAR \times SCALAR \to SCALAR$
$\_ \times \_ : SCALAR \times SCALAR \to SCALAR$

(definitions omitted)

$[EDGES]$

$(\_ \cdot v1), (\_ \cdot v2), (\_ \cdot v3), (\_ \cdot v4) : EDGES \to VECTOR$

$\forall edges : EDGES \bullet$
$\quad edges \cdot v1 + edges \cdot v2 + edges \cdot v3 + edges \cdot v4 = 0$

(further definitions omitted)

$[SHEAR]$

Here *VECTOR, SCALAR, ANGLE, EDGES* and *SHEAR* are given sets; $+$, $|\ |$, and $\cdot$ are respectively vector addition, module and product; cos^{-1}, $/$ and $\times$ are cosine inverse, scalar division and scalar multiplication; the operations $\cdot v1$, $\cdot v2$, $\cdot v3$ and $\cdot v4$ yield vectors out of edges. The full definitions of these operations have been omitted because they would add little to this example.

The module *Quadrilateral* that follows comprises the definitions of all classes used in this example. As these classes are closely related it is more natural to specify them together rather than separately.

Quadrilaterals[$P :: Vector$]

A quadrilateral object has two attributes, namely *edges* and *position*. The former represents the four sides that all quadrilaterals have, and the latter its current position. A method *Move* is provided to allow changes of position.

> *Class Quadrilateral*
>
> > *State*
> > $edges : EDGES$
> > $position : VECTOR$
>
> > *Move*
> > $\Delta position$
> > $move? : VECTOR$
> >
> > $position' = position + move?$

The class *Parallelogram* inherits from *Quadrilateral*, so parallelograms have the same attributes and can be manipulated with the same methods as quadrilaterals. Moreover a class invariant has been added to it stating that all parallelograms have opposite sides of equal length. Also, one may inquire what the angle between the first and second edge is. Note that the other angles can be easily calculated from this one.

> *Class Parallelogram* $<$ *Quadrilateral*
>
> > *State*
> > $edges \cdot v1 + edges \cdot v3 = 0$
>
> > *Angle*
> > $a! : ANGLE$
> >
> > $a! = cos^{-1}((edges \cdot v1) \cdot (edges \cdot v2)\ /\ |edges \cdot v1| \times |edges \cdot v1|)$

The class *Rhombus* inherits from *Parallelogram*. However a new predicate has been conjoined to the inherited class invariant stating that in addition rhombi have adjacent sides of the same length.

> *Class Rhombus* < *Parallelogram*
>> *State*
>> $|edges.v1| = |edges.v2|$

The specification of the *Rectangle* class states that every rectangle is a parallelogram with perpendicular adjacent sides. The method *Angle* has been redefined in a more concise way.

> *Class Rectangle* < *Parallelogram*
>> *State*
>> $(edges.v1).(edges.v2) = 0$
>>
>> *Angle*
>> $a! : ANGLE$
>> $a! = \pi/2$

Every *Square* object is both a *Rhombus* and a *Rectangle* object.

Class Square < *Rhombus, Rectangle*

A shearable quadrilateral is a quadrilateral that can be sheared.

> *Class ShearableQuadrilateral* < *Quadrilateral*
>> *Shear*
>> $\Delta edges, position$
>> $s? : SHEAR$
>>
>> **(definitions omitted)**

A shearable parallelogram is both a shearable quadrilateral and a parallelogram.

Class ShearableParallelogram < *ShearableQuadrilateral, Parallelogram*

Because OOZE objects have unique identifiers and are organized into meta-classes, what has indeed been specified is a system in which objects can be created, modified and deleted. Moreover it is easy to define a method that outputs all quadrilaterals created so far,

$QuadsList \equiv \overline{Quadrilateral.objs}$

where $\overline{Quadrilateral}$ is the unique object of the *Quadrilateral* meta-class, and *objs* is the attribute of that class that contains the current list of all quadrilaterals. In a context where *Quadrilateral* is the most specialized class, we could write just $QuadsList \equiv objs$.

7.3 Button Example

In the executable OOZE specification that follows 'self' refers to the very object upon which a method is currently acting, and the semantics of the free types *MOUSE_LOCATION*, *MOUSE_CLICK* and *STATUS* is taken to be the class of initial algebras that correspond to those types respectively. Therefore *In* and *Out*, *Up*, *Primed* and *Ignored*, and *On* and *Off* are the only elements that those respective types have. Details of the semantics of OOZE can be found in [Alencar and Goguen 1991].

Theory ButtonStates

[*ACTION*, *NAME*]

$MOUSE\_LOCATION ::= In\,|\,Out$
$MOUSE\_CLICK ::= Up\,|\,Primed\,|\,Ignored$
$STATUS ::= On\,|\,Off$

Here *ACTION* and *NAME* are given sets.

Buttons[*P* :: *ButtonStates*]

Class Button

A button has two attributes, namely *loc* and *click*, that respectively record the mouse location and if the mouse button is either released, depressed or being ignored.

State

loc : *MOUSE_LOCATION*
click : *MOUSE_CLICK*

Initially the mouse is outside the button's active area and its button is released.

Init

$loc' = Out$
$click' = Up$

If the mouse button is released the screen button records this fact and provides no actions to be executed.

```
┌─ MouseUp ──────────────────────────────────────────────
│ Δclick
│ act! : Seq ACTION
│ ────────────────────────────────────────────────────────
│ act! = ⟨⟩
│ click' = Up
└─────────────────────────────────────────────────────────
```

What the screen button records when the mouse button is depressed depends on the mouse location.

```
┌─ MouseDown ────────────────────────────────────────────
│ Δclick
│ ────────────────────────────────────────────────────────
│ click' = Primed   if loc = In
│ ────────────────────────────────────────────────────────
│ click' = Ignored  if loc = Out
└─────────────────────────────────────────────────────────
```

The mouse may leave the screen button's active area.

```
┌─ MouseLeave ───────────────────────────────────────────
│ Δloc
│ ────────────────────────────────────────────────────────
│ loc' = Out
└─────────────────────────────────────────────────────────
```

The mouse may enter the screen button's active area.

```
┌─ MouseEnter ───────────────────────────────────────────
│ Δloc
│ ────────────────────────────────────────────────────────
│ loc' = In
└─────────────────────────────────────────────────────────
```

```
┌─ Class Action < Button ────────────────────────────────
```

An *Action* button is a *Button* with a sequence of actions to be executed when it is activated.

```
┌─ State ────────────────────────────────────────────────
│ action : Seq ACTION
└─────────────────────────────────────────────────────────
```

One must provide the sequence of actions.

```
┌─ Init ─────────────────────────────────────────────────
│ act? : Seq ACTION
│ ────────────────────────────────────────────────────────
│ action' = act?
└─────────────────────────────────────────────────────────
```

A sequence of actions to be executed is provided if the mouse's button is released in the *Action* button's active area.

```
┌─ MouseUp ────────────────────────────────────────────
│ Δclick
│ act! : Seq ACTION
│ ─────────────────────────────────────────────────────
│ click' = Up, act! = ⟨⟩
│    if click = Ignored
│ ─────────────────────────────────────────────────────
│ click' = Up, act! = action
│    if click = Primed
└──────────────────────────────────────────────────────
```

```
┌─ Class On-Off < Button ──────────────────────────────
│
│ An On-Off button is a Button that can be switched on or off.
│
│ ┌─ State ───────────────────────────────────────────
│ │ status : STATUS
│ └───────────────────────────────────────────────────
│
│ One must provide the button's initial status.
│
│ ┌─ Init ────────────────────────────────────────────
│ │ status? : STATUS
│ │ ──────────────────────────────────────────────────
│ │ status' = status
│ └───────────────────────────────────────────────────
└──────────────────────────────────────────────────────
```

```
┌─ Class Toggle < On-Off ──────────────────────────────
│
│ A Toggle button is an On-Off button that changes its status if the mouse button is
│ released in its active area.
│
│ switch : STATUS → STATUS
│ ──────────────────────────────────────────────────────
│ ∀ s : STATUS •
│     switch(s) = On   if  s = Off
│     switch(s) = Off  if  s = On
```

MouseUp _____

$\Delta click, status$
$act! : \text{Seq } ACTION$

$click' = Up, status' = switch(status), act! = \langle\rangle$
  $\underline{if} click = Primed$

$click' = Up, status' = status, act! = \langle\rangle$
  $\underline{if} click = Ignored$

Class Radio < Action, On-Off _____

A *Radio* button is a button that is concurrently an *Action* and an *On-Off* button, and that belongs to a cluster.

State _____

$cluster\_name : NAME$

Initially one must identify the cluster to which the *Radio* button belongs.

Init _____

$cluster\_name? : NAME$

$cluster\_name' = cluster\_name?$

The consequences of releasing the mouse button in the *Radio* button's active area depend upon whether the mouse button is being ignored, and the current status.

MouseUp _____

$\Delta click, status$
$act! : \text{Seq } ACTION$

$click' = Up, status' = status, act! = \langle\rangle$
  $\underline{if} click = Ignored$

$click' = Up, status' = On, act! = action$
  $\underline{if} status = Off \wedge click = Primed$

$click' = Up, status = On, act! = \langle\rangle$
  $\underline{if} status = On \wedge click = Primed$

A *Radio* button can be asked to switch off.

TurnOff _____

$\Delta status$

$status' = Off$

If the radio status is *On* the auxiliary method *cluster_members* yields all other *Radio* buttons that belong to the same cluster, otherwise an empty set of *Radio* objects is yeilded.

$cluster\_members$: Seq $Radio \times Radio \rightarrow$ **P** $Radio$

$\forall S$: Seq $Radio$; r_1, r_2 : $Radio \bullet$
$\quad cluster\_members(\langle r_1 \rangle \frown S, r_2) = \{r_1\} \cup cluster\_members(S, r_2)$
$\qquad \underline{if}\ r_1 \cdot cluster\_name = r_2 \cdot cluster\_name \wedge r_2 \cdot status = On \wedge r_1 \neq r_2$
$\quad cluster\_members(\langle r_1 \rangle \frown S, r_2) = cluster\_members(S, r_2)$
$\qquad \underline{if}\ r_1 \cdot cluster\_name \neq r_2 \cdot cluster\_name \vee r_2 \cdot status = Off \vee r_1 = r_2$
$\quad cluster\_members(\langle \rangle, r_2) = \{\}$

All other buttons in the same cluster can be asked to switch off. Note that 'self' refers to the specific object upon which a method is currently acting.

$TurnOthersOff \equiv Map(cluster\_members(objs, cluster\_name) \setminus self, TurnOff)$

The actions that result from the release of the mouse's button can reflect on the whole cluster if this is convenient.

$ClusterMouseUp \equiv MouseUp \mathbin{\raise.2ex\hbox{$\,;\,$}} TurnOthersOff$

Here $\mathbin{\raise.2ex\hbox{$\,;\,$}}$ is sequential method composition. Therefore $m1 \mathbin{\raise.2ex\hbox{$\,;\,$}} m2$ indicates that first $m1$ is applied, and after that $m2$.

Observe that *Radio* buttons have been organized in clusters, and that the attribute *cluster_name* refers to the unique cluster to which a *Radio* button belongs. In the *Radio* class, the operation *cluster_members* yields the set of all radios that belong to a certain cluster, *TurnOthersOff* turns off all *Radio* buttons except the one that it receives as a parameter, and *ClusterMouseUp* switches off the other buttons in the same cluster if the one that it receives as a parameter is switched on.

Moreover, although only an executable specification of the Button system is currently presented, a non-executable OOZE theory, where the axioms can be arbitrary first order sentences, could have been used to specify a similar system. For example if a theory were actually used, the method *MouseUp* of class *Action* could have been defined as follows

---

MouseUp
$\Delta click$
$act!$: Seq $ACTION$

$click' = Up \wedge ((act! = \langle \rangle \wedge click = Ignored) \vee (act! = action \wedge click = Primed))$

The reasons for preferring our executable specification for the Button system are several. First, it supports rapid prototyping. This can greatly improve communication with the client, and confidence that the desired system behaviour has been captured. Second, at least in this case, the more limited form of the executable axioms makes the specifications easier to understand and to update, as pre-conditions are clearly distinguished from post-conditions. Moreover, much of what is specified in Z and other languages based upon it, although written in a non-executable form, is actually executable or else can be made so with minor changes. For example, compare the non-executable version of the method *MouseUp* above with its executable version presented in the specification of the Button system.

7.4   Conclusion

OOZE is a 'wide spectrum' object oriented language with both *loose* specifications and *executable* (compilable or interpretable) programs. These two aspects of the language can be encapsulated in *modules* and may be linked by *views*, which assert refinement relationships.

Modules are organized according to an *import hierarchy*, and can also be generic, that is, *parameterized*. A system of modules, which may be loose and can even have empty bodies, can be used to express the large-grain *design* of a system. A single, very high level module can be used to express overall *requirements*, via a view to a module that encapsulates the whole system, or at earlier stages of development, just its design or specification.

Rapid prototypes can be developed and precisely linked to their specifications and requirements by views. The use of loose specifications to define interfaces can be seen as a powerful semantic type system [Goguen 1991]. Theorem proving can be provided for OOZE by the 2OBJ system [Goguen *et al.* 1992a], which is itself an extension of OBJ3. OOZE is truly object oriented, allowing varying number of objects to a class, and complex objects (that is, object valued attributes), as well as multiple inheritance and dynamic binding. The precise semantics based on order sorted algebra supports exception handling and overloaded operations. Objects are organized into meta-classes that allow operations ranging over instances of a class. These characteristics are unique among the proposals for extending Z, and along with its animation and database facilities, make OOZE a very attractive language for developing large systems. More about OOZE can be found in [Alencar and Goguen 1991].

8

Schuman & Pitt Approach

8.1 Schuman & Pitt Notation Overview

The Schuman and Pitt approach is described in [Schuman and Pitt 1987], [Schuman *et al.* 1990]. The notation of Schuman and Pitt is described in published papers as object oriented. In fact it is more concerned with fundamental issues of composition of schemas and reasoning about the resulting composition than with specifying object oriented systems, or specifying systems in an object oriented way. However, its principle of specifying no more than is required (so, for example, it is not necessary to say that everything else stays the same for most operation schemas) does make it particularly useful for specifying systems that consist of lots of small states, operated on by local operations, and then composed together to form the total system state.

The state schema has three parts: state component declarations, the state invariant predicate and the initialization condition predicate:

```
┌─ State ──────────────────────────────────────────
│  state component declarations
│  ─────────────────────────────
│  state invariant predicate
│  ─────────────────────────────
│  initialization condition predicate
└──────────────────────────────────────────────────
```

Corresponding operation (or event) schemas also have three components: input and output parameter declarations, the pre-condition predicate, and the post-condition predicate: If a predicate part is omitted, it defaults to *true*.

```
┌─ State.Op(params) ───────────────────────────────
│  parameter declarations
│  ─────────────────────────────
│  pre-condition predicate
│  ─────────────────────────────
│  post-condition predicate
└──────────────────────────────────────────────────
```

By convention, the name of an operation schema is the state schema name followed by the operation name. Then the corresponding state component declarations and state invariant predicate are implicitly included in operation schema.

8.2   Quadrilateral Example

This section introduces the Schuman and Pitt approach by respecifying the quadrilaterals example.

The Quadrilateral example uses some of the things specified in section 2.2. A Quadrilateral is defined by five vectors, four edges and a position:

```
┌─ Quad ─────────────────────────────────────────
│ v1, v2, v3, v4 : Vector
│ position : Vector
├────────────────────────────────────────────────
│ v1 + v2 + v3 + v4 = 0
└────────────────────────────────────────────────
```

We can move and shear a quadrilateral, by supplying the relevant input parameters:

```
┌─ Quad.Move(move) ──────────────────────────────
│ move : Vector
├════════════════════════════════════════════════
│ position' = position + move
└────────────────────────────────────────────────
```

```
┌─ Quad.Shear(s) ────────────────────────────────
│ s : Shear
├════════════════════════════════════════════════
│ definition omitted
└────────────────────────────────────────────────
```

Note that in the post-condition we do not have to say that everything else stays the same. This is supplied by the semantics in terms of *historical inference*.

8.2.1   Parallelograms

We can inherit from the general *Quad* to get a *Parallelogram* by adding an extra constraint (we could also add extra state variables). The constraint is that opposite sides are of equal length and parallel.

```
┌─ Parallelogram ────────────────────────────────
│ Quad
├────────────────────────────────────────────────
│ v1 + v3 = 0
└────────────────────────────────────────────────
```

Note that the new condition $v1 + v3 = 0$ together with the state invariant $v1 + v2 + v3 + v4 = 0$ imply that $v2 + v4 = 0$.

Operations must be inherited explicitly. All conditions, pre and post, may be strengthened. If the pre-condition is strengthened it implies that we could not necessarily use a *Parallelogram* wherever we could use a *Quad*. But note that if we *can* use it, then it behaves in a way that is consistent with the behaviour of a *Quad*.

```
__Parallelogram.Move_____
  Quad.Move

_____
```

```
__Parallelogram.Shear_____
  Quad.Shear

_____
```

Parallelogram has a new operation, enquiring about the angle between adjacent sides (the arrow shows that *a* is an output parameter):

```
__Parallelogram.Angle(→ a)_____
  a : Angle
  ═══════════════════════════════════════════════
  a = cos⁻¹(v1.v2/ | v1 | | v2 |)
```

$$a = \cos^{-1}(v1.v2/ \mid v1 \mid \mid v2 \mid)$$

Note again how we do not have to say that all the state components are unchanged by this operation.

8.2.2 Rhombus

We can further inherit and add another constraint to turn a parallelogram into a rhombus by constraining adjacent sides to be the same length:

```
__Rhombus_____
  Parallelogram
  _____
  | v1 |=| v2 |
```

The Move and Angle operations are inherited without change.

```
__Rhombus.Move_____
  Parallelogram.Move

_____
```

```
__Rhombus.Angle(→ a)_____
  Parallelogram.Angle(→ a)

_____
```

It is not appropriate to shear a rhombus (the state invariant cannot be met) so no such operation is defined.

8.2.3 Rectangle

Alternatively, we can inherit and add another constraint to turn a parallelogram into a rectangle by constraining the angle between adjacent sides to be a right angle.

```
┌─ Rectangle ──────────────────────────────────
│ Parallelogram
├──────────────
│ v1.v2 = 0
│
└──────────────────────────────────────────────
```

The Move operation is inherited without change.

```
┌─ Rectangle.Move ─────────────────────────────
│ Parallelogram.Move
│
└──────────────────────────────────────────────
```

Rather than inherit the form of the Parallelogram angle operation, we can redefine it:

```
┌─ Rectangle.Angle(→ a) ───────────────────────
│ a : Angle
├══════════════
│ a = π/2
│
└──────────────────────────────────────────────
```

8.2.4 Square

We can inherit from two parents to get a square

```
┌─ Square ─────────────────────────────────────
│ Rhombus
│ Rectangle
│
└──────────────────────────────────────────────
```

We could inherit the move operation from either parent.

```
┌─ Square.Move ────────────────────────────────
│ Rhombus.Move
│
└──────────────────────────────────────────────
```

The angle operation is more appropriately inherited from the Rectangle:

```
┌─ Square.Angle(→ a) ──────────────────────────
│ Rectangle.Angle(→ a)
│
└──────────────────────────────────────────────
```

8.2.5 Promotion

We define a set of quadrilaterals to include a special one representing the selected quadrilateral. All the promoted operations act on this selected quadrilateral.

```
┌─ SetOfQuad ──────────────────────────────────
│ q : P Quad
│ selected : Quad
├──────────────
│ selected ∈ q
├══════════════
│ q = ∅
│
└──────────────────────────────────────────────
```

We can select a chosen quadrilateral from a set, and apply an operation to this one element, promoting the operation up to work on the larger state.

```
┌─ SetOfQuad.Select(s) ──────────────────────────────────
│ s : Quad
├────────────────────────────────────────────────────────
│ s ∈ q
├────────────────────────────────────────────────────────
│ selected = s
└────────────────────────────────────────────────────────
```

```
┌─ SetOfQuad.Move(move) ─────────────────────────────────
│ move : Vector
│ selected.Move(move)
└────────────────────────────────────────────────────────
```

8.3   Button Example

This section further explains the Schuman and Pitt approach, by respecifying the button example.

8.3.1   General Buttons

A general button has two state components, *loc* (initially *Out*) and *click* (initially *Up*):

```
┌─ Button ───────────────────────────────────────────────
│ loc : MouseLocation
│ click : MouseButton
├────────────────────────────────────────────────────────
│ loc' = Out
│ click' = Up
└────────────────────────────────────────────────────────
```

The mouse operations are similar to the Z definitions:

```
┌─ Button.MouseUp ───────────────────────────────────────
│ click ≠ Up
├────────────────────────────────────────────────────────
│ click' = Up
└────────────────────────────────────────────────────────
```

```
┌─ Button.MouseDown ─────────────────────────────────────
│ click = Up
├────────────────────────────────────────────────────────
│ (loc = In ∧ click' = Primed) ∨ (loc = Out ∧ click' = Ignored)
└────────────────────────────────────────────────────────
```

Note that in this variant of Z we are not required to say that 'everything else stays the same', as we are usually. This does, however, mean that we are forced to make an explicit decision about whether the change of click (to *Primed* or *Ignored*) occurs based on the location of the mouse before this operation, or after. In plain Z, we explicitly say that $loc' = loc$, so the question is immaterial. But here, a parallel composition of this operation with another may alter loc, and so whether we base our decision on loc or loc' makes a difference. We choose the before state.

$$
\begin{array}{l}
\underline{\hspace{0.5em}Button.MouseEnter\hspace{8em}} \\
\;\; loc = Out \\
\rule{8em}{0.4pt} \\
\;\; loc' = In
\end{array}
$$

$$
\begin{array}{l}
\underline{\hspace{0.5em}Button.MouseLeave\hspace{8em}} \\
\;\; loc = In \\
\rule{8em}{0.4pt} \\
\;\; loc' = Out
\end{array}
$$

8.3.2   Action Buttons

Action buttons send out a set of actions when they are clicked. In this instance, 'clicked' means that it undergoes a *MouseUp* when the mouse is currently *Primed* (that is, the mouse was clicked in the button, and is now being released in the button).

An action button is the same as a general button, except for an extra state component to store the actions that it sends out. These actions are set up at initialization.

$$
\begin{array}{l}
\underline{\hspace{0.5em}ActionButton\hspace{8em}} \\
\;\; Button \\
\;\; act : \mathbf{P}\, ACTION \\

\end{array}
$$

$$
\begin{array}{l}
\underline{\hspace{0.5em}ActionButton.Init(\,a\,)\hspace{6em}} \\
\;\; a : \mathbf{P}\, ACTION \\
\rule{8em}{0.4pt} \\
\;\; act' = a
\end{array}
$$

Primed *MouseUp* outputs the actions it has stored internally. If it is ignoring the *MouseUp*, it outputs the empty set of actions. This is a bit spurious, but like the Z version, it is not possible for outputs to occur under some circumstances but not occur under others.

$$
\begin{array}{l}
\underline{\hspace{0.5em}ActionButton.MouseUp(\rightarrow a\,)\hspace{4em}} \\
\;\; Button.MouseUp \\
\;\; a : \mathbf{P}\, ACTION \\
\rule{8em}{0.4pt} \\
\;\; (click = Primed \wedge a = act) \vee (click = Ignored \wedge a = \varnothing)
\end{array}
$$

The remaining actions are directly inherited from the parent, but this does have to be explicitly stated.

┌─ *ActionButton.MouseDown* ─────────────────────────────
│ *Button.MouseDown*
│
└──

┌─ *ActionButton.MouseLeave* ────────────────────────────
│ *Button.MouseLeave*
│
└──

┌─ *ActionButton.MouseEnter* ────────────────────────────
│ *Button.MouseEnter*
│
└──

8.3.3 On Off Buttons

These buttons have an additional state variable, which in general is visually represented as a 'tick', or a darkening, or some other indication that the button is 'on'. The exact behaviour of the button is described in the children of OnOffButton; here we just inherit Button's definitions for the change of *loc* and *click*.

┌─ *OnOffButton* ──
│ *Button*
│ *status : Status*
│
└──

┌─ *OnOffButton.MouseUp* ────────────────────────────────
│ *Button.MouseUp*
│
└──

┌─ *OnOffButton.MouseDown* ──────────────────────────────
│ *Button.MouseDown*
│
└──

┌─ *OnOffButton.MouseLeave* ─────────────────────────────
│ *Button.MouseLeave*
│
└──

┌─ *OnOffButton.MouseEnter* ─────────────────────────────
│ *Button.MouseEnter*
│
└──

8.3.4 Toggle Buttons

Toggle buttons are OnOff buttons that switch between their two states in response to a *MouseUp* when *Primed*. Clicking on the button when they are on turns them off, and when off turns them back on.

When they are initialized, they are *Off*.

┌─ *ToggleButton* ───────────────────────────────────────
│ *OnOffButton*
├──
│ $status' = Off$
│
└──

```
  ┌─ ToggleButton.MouseUp ──────────────────────────────────
  │ Button.MouseUp
  │ ══════════════════════════════════════════════════════
  │ (click = Primed ∧ status′ ≠ status)
  │ ∨ (click = Ignored ∧ status′ = status)
  └───────────────────────────────────────────────────────
```

The remaining actions are inherited directly.

```
  ┌─ ToggleButton.MouseDown ────────────────────────────────
  │ Button.MouseDown
  └───────────────────────────────────────────────────────
```

```
  ┌─ ToggleButton.MouseEnter ───────────────────────────────
  │ Button.MouseEnter
  └───────────────────────────────────────────────────────
```

```
  ┌─ ToggleButton.MouseLeave ───────────────────────────────
  │ Button.MouseLeave
  └───────────────────────────────────────────────────────
```

8.3.5   Radio Buttons

Radio buttons are OnOff buttons in that they have an internal state that can be either on or off. They come in clusters so that of all the buttons in a cluster, only one is on at a time. If another button in the cluster is clicked, it goes on, and the previously on button goes off. Clicking a button that is already on causes no change.

There are two ways of modelling Radio buttons. The first is to model a cluster as one object, with a self-consistent state. The second is to model the Radio buttons as individual objects, which must then communicate with each other in order to keep in step.

We must be able to identify individual buttons independently of their current state, which at the moment we cannot do. We therefore introduce a set of button identifiers.

[*ButtonID*]

Following the first approach of specifying clusters of Radio buttons, a Radio cluster has a distinguished button, which is the one that is currently On. This changes with mouse clicks.

```
  ┌─ RadioCluster ──────────────────────────────────────────
  │ button : ButtonID ⇸ OnOffButton
  │ on : ButtonID
  │ ═══════════════════════════════════════════════════════
  │ on ∈ dom button
  │ button(on).status = On
  │ ∀ b : dom button | b ≠ on • button(b).status = Off
  └───────────────────────────────────────────────────────
```

Mouse events must now pass a button identifier as a parameter.

RadioCluster.MouseUp(b)

b : dom *button*

$button(b).click \neq Up$

$button(b).click = Up$
$(button(b).click = Primed \wedge on = b) \vee (button(b).click = Ignored)$

RadioCluster.MouseDown(b)

b : dom *button*

$button(b).click = Up$

$(button(b).loc = In \wedge button(b).click = Primed)$
$\vee (button(b).loc = Out \wedge button(b).click = Ignored)$

The above definitions define the behaviour from scratch. It is also possible to use the previously defined operations on buttons and promote them to work on the larger state. The 'everything else stays the same' semantics makes this particularly easy. We do this by obtaining the smaller piece of state and then applying the operation to it with the dot notation.

RadioCluster.MouseUp(b)

b : dom *button*
$button(b).MouseUp$

$(button(b).click = Primed \wedge on = b) \vee (button(b).click = Ignored)$

RadioCluster.MouseDown(b)

b : dom *button*
$button(b).MouseDown$

MouseLeave and *MouseEnter* can be treated similarly.

Following the second approach, a Radio button can be described in its own, but must output actions to turn off the other button in the cluster. Hence it is an action button, too.

RadioButton

OnOffButton
ActionButton

However, the behaviour on *MouseUp* cannot be specified by inheriting from *Action.MouseUp*, because of the stricter condition which needs to be satisfied before the actions can be output (now also requiring status to be off) occurring in one branch of the 'or' condition:

RadioButton.MouseUp($\rightarrow a$)
OnOff.MouseUp
$a : \mathbf{P}\ ACTION$

$(\quad clicked = Primed \wedge status = Off \wedge a = act$
$\vee \quad ((clicked = Primed \wedge status = On) \vee clicked = Ignored) \wedge a = \varnothing)$
$status' = On$

An on radio button may also be asked to turn off:

RadioButton.TurnOff
$status = On$

$status' = Off$

9

Z++

Kevin C. Lano[1]

9.1 Z++ Notation Overview

The two case studies are specified in Z++, to highlight the differences and similarities between the specification styles possible in this language and in the other object-oriented extensions to Z. A full description of the Z++ language is contained in [Lano and Haughton 1991], and is also described in [Lano 1991]. Here we give only an overview of the syntax.

A Z++ specification is a sequence of Z++ paragraphs, where a paragraph is either a Z paragraph (text item, schema, axiomatic definition, and so forth), in which a class name can be used as a type, and class methods as operations or schemas, as described below, or is a class definition. The BNF description of a Z++ class declaration is:

$$
\begin{aligned}
Object\_Class \quad &::= \text{CLASS } Identifier\ TypeParameters \\
&\quad [\text{EXTENDS } Imported] \\
&\quad [\text{TYPES } Types] \\
&\quad [\text{FUNCTIONS } Axdefs] \\
&\quad [\text{OWNS } Locals] \\
&\quad [\text{INVARIANT } Predicate] \\
&\quad [\text{RETURNS } Optypes] \\
&\quad [\text{OPERATIONS } Optypes] \\
&\quad [\text{ACTIONS } Acts] \\
&\quad \text{END CLASS}
\end{aligned}
$$

$$
\begin{aligned}
TypeParameters &::= [\ Parlist\ ] \\
&\quad |\ \ \epsilon
\end{aligned}
$$

$$
Imported \quad ::= Idlist
$$

$$
\begin{aligned}
Parlist \quad &::= Identifier\ [,\ Parlist\ ] \\
&\quad |\ \ Identifier \ll Identifier\ [,\ Parlist\ ]
\end{aligned}
$$

$$
Types \quad ::= Type\_Declarations
$$

---

[1] Oxford University Computing Laboratory, Programming Research Group, 8–11 Keble Road, Oxford, OX1 3QD. Current address: Performance Technology, Lloyds Register of Shipping, 29 Wellesley Road, Croydon, CR0 2AJ.

Locals	$::=$ *Identifier* : *Type* ; *Locals*
	$\mid$ *Identifier* : *Type*
Optypes	$::=$ *Identifier* : *Idlist* $\rightarrow$ *Idlist* ; *Optypes*
	$\mid$ *Identifier* : *Idlist* $\rightarrow$ *Idlist*
Acts	$::=$ [*Expression* &] *Identifier Idlist* $==>$ *Code* ; *Acts*
	$\mid$ [*Expression* &] *Identifier Idlist* $==>$ *Code*

The *TypeParameters* are a list (possibly empty) of *generic* type parameters used in the class definition. A parameter X can be required to be a descendent of a class A via the notation $A \ll X$ here.

The **EXTENDS** list is the set of previously defined classes that we are incorporating into this class. The *Types* are type declarations of type identifiers used in declarations of the local variables of the object. The *Local* variable declarations are attribute declarations, in the style of variable declarations in Z. The **OPERATIONS** list declares the types of the operations, as functions from a sequence of input domains to an output domain. The **RETURNS** list of operations defines the output type of those attributes and functions of the objects internal state that are externally visible; these are operations with no side-effect on the state, and it has been found helpful in practice [Zimmer 1990] to distinguish these from operations that do change the state. The **INVARIANT** gives a predicate that specifies the properties of the internal state, in terms of the local variables of the object. This predicate is guaranteed to be true of the state of an object class instance between executions of the operations of the object instance.

The **ACTIONS** list the definitions of the various operations that can be performed on instances of the object; for instance we would write:

$$READ \; x \;\; ==> \;\; q' = tail \; q \wedge x = head \; q$$

in a specification of queues with contents q.

The input parameters are listed before the output parameters in the action definitions. *Code* includes Z predicates and procedural UNIFORM [Stanley-Smith and Cahill 1990] code, both have a precise semantics as predicate transformers: for any piece of code C in the scope of a declaration D there is a corresponding predicate $\theta_{C,D}$ such that the predicate transformer semantics of C and $\theta_{C,D}$ are the same under D [Lano and Breuer 1990].

Alternative forms of syntax are possible, and have been developed. A Z^{++} specification can be printed out using the Object-Z macros (an 'Object-Z' style), or using a style which combines Z schema boxes with C style function definitions (a 'C++ style'). These outputs are supported by our toolset.

A Z^{++} specification is similar in design to a Z specification in that it consists of a sequence of Z^{++} paragraphs, of which some can be class definitions. Class definitions correspond to a more restricted sequence of paragraphs, providing a standardized format in order to ease comprehension.

9.2   Quadrilaterals

At the top level of this specification are given sets of vectors and scalars:

[*Vector, Scalar*]

together with definitions of the vector operations $+$, $|\ |$, $\cdot$, and so forth:

$$\begin{array}{|l} \_ + \_ : Vector \times Vector \rightarrow Vector \\ \mathbf{0} : Vector \end{array}$$

$$\begin{array}{|l} anticos : Scalar \rightarrow Angle \\ \_/\_ : Scalar \times Scalar \rightarrow Scalar \end{array}$$

as in the Z specification.

$$\begin{array}{|l} \_Edges \underline{\hspace{8cm}} \\ v1, v2, v3, v4 : Vector \\ \hline (v1 + v2) + (v3 + v4) = \mathbf{0} \end{array}$$

We specify a quadrilateral in two stages:

```
CLASS Quad0
OWNS
 edges   :  Edges;
 position  :  Vector
OPERATIONS
 Move  :  Vector  →
ACTIONS
 Move move?   ==>   position' = position + move?
END CLASS
```

This class defines a set of objects with two attributes *edges* and *position*, and with one admissible operation *Move*. In the definition of the operation, we have the implicit statement that $edges' = edges$, since $edges'$ does not occur in the predicate of the definition, and that the invariant of the class is maintained.

$$\begin{array}{|l} shear : Shear \times Edges \rightarrow Edges \end{array}$$

We omit details of this operation.

```
CLASS Quad EXTENDS Quad0
OPERATIONS
 ShearQuad  :  Shear  →
ACTIONS
 ShearQuad s?   ==>   edges' = shear(s?, edges)
END CLASS
```

The *ShearQuad* operation changes only the *edges* attribute. The context of the class creates the precondition $edges \in Edges \wedge shear(s?, edges) \in Edges$ for this operation.

We have: $Quad0 \sqsubseteq Quad$: $Quad$ is a refinement of $Quad0$ [Lano and Haughton 1992].

```
CLASS Parallelogram EXTENDS Quad
INVARIANT
   edges.v1  +  edges.v3  =  0
RETURNS
 AngleQuad  :   →  Angle
ACTIONS
 AngleQuad  ==>  anticos((edges.v1 · edges.v2)/(| edges.v1 || edges.v2 |))
END CLASS
```

We do not have $Quad \sqsubseteq Parallelogram$, since the preconditions of the *Move* and *ShearQuad* operations have been restricted in *Parallelogram* by the extra invariant.

We can document properties of the *Parallelogram* class by means of algebraic constraints:

$$\forall\, p : Parallelogram;\; m, n : Vector\; \bullet$$
$$(AngleQuad((Move\; p)m)) = (AngleQuad\; p)$$
$$(Move(Move\; p)n)m = (Move\; p)(m + n)$$

valid under observational equivalence with respect to visibility of all attributes.

The general format for writing a call of a method Op to a class instance a, with input parameters x and output parameters y, is:

$$(Op\; a)x = (y, a')$$

where a' represents the modified instance. In the case of a returnable property Op, a' can be omitted, since $a' = a$. Likewise, if the operation has no outputs, then y can be omitted. Methods can also be used as schemas, within a class in which the state transformed by the method is visible (that is, the method must be defined in the class or in an ancestor class. Ambiguities in naming are resolved by prefixing the method name by the class whose definition of the method we want to take in the schema).

```
CLASS Rhombus EXTENDS Parallelogram
INVARIANT
 | edges.v1 |  =  | edges.v2 |
END CLASS
```

We have $\neg\,(Parallelogram \sqsubseteq Rhombus)$, since the requirement that *ShearQuad* preserves the condition that the *edges* form a rhombus implies that $s? = 0$ (given the natural definition of *shear*). However, we could base *Rhombus* instead on $Quad0$.

```
CLASS Rectangle EXTENDS Parallelogram
INVARIANT
  (edges.v1) · (edges.v2) = 0
END CLASS
```

```
CLASS Square EXTENDS Parallelogram
INVARIANT
  (edges.v1) · (edges.v2) = 0
  | edges.v1 | = | edges.v2 |
END CLASS
```

The class *Rectangle* is a refinement of *Square*, via the mapping *sq* which maps a rectangle to the square with sides equal to the shortest side of the rectangle. Similarly, *Rhombus* and *Rectangle* are refinements of *Parallelogram* (without the *ShearQuad* operation). These are anomalies caused by the operations which are valid for these classes. Since a refinement f of a function op_1 to a function op_2 has the property that:

$$(f\,v, x) \in \text{dom } op_1 \wedge (f\,v', x') \in \text{dom } op_1 \wedge op_2(v, x) = op_2(v', x') \Rightarrow$$
$$op_1(f\,v, x) = op_1(f\,v', x')$$

we can deduce that any f which fails to have this property cannot be a refinement - in particular an operation op_1 on squares which returns the length of the perimeter does not refine to a similar operation on rectangles (two rectangles with the same perimeter can map to squares with different perimeter).

As in the Object-Z specification, we need a set of identifiers for quadrilaterals:

[*QID*]

which are used to reference the quadrilaterals used by the drawing system:

```
CLASS DrawingSystem
OWNS
  screen  :  QID  ⇸  Quad
RETURNS
  LookupQuad  :  QID  →  Quad;
  ANGLE  :  QID  →  Angle
OPERATIONS
  AddQuad  :  Quad  →  QID;
  DeleteQuad  :  QID  →;
  UpdateQuad  :  QID  Quad  →;
  MOVE  :  QID  Vector  →;
  SHEAR  :  QID  Shear  →
ACTIONS
  LookupQuad qid? quad!  ==>  qid? ∈ dom screen ∧
                              quad! = screen(qid?);
  ANGLE qid? angle!  ==>  angle! = (AngleQuad screen(qid?));

  AddQuad quad? qid!  ==>  qid! ∉ dom screen ∧
                           screen' = screen ∪ { qid! ↦ quad? };
```

$$DeleteQuad \ qid? \quad ==> \quad qid? \ \in \ \text{dom} \ screen \ \wedge$$
$$screen' \ = \ \{qid?\} \ \lhd \ screen;$$
$$UpdateQuad \ qid? \ q' \ ==> \quad qid? \ \in \ \text{dom} \ screen \ \wedge$$
$$screen' \ = \ screen \ \oplus \ \{qid? \ \mapsto \ q'\};$$
$$MOVE \ qid? \ vec? \quad ==> \quad q' \ = \ (Move \ screen(qid?)) \ vec? \ \wedge$$
$$UpdateQuad;$$
$$SHEAR \ qid? \ s? \ ==> \quad q' \ = \ (ShearQuad \ screen(qid?)) \ s? \ \wedge$$
$$UpdateQuad$$

END CLASS

In this class *UpdateQuad* is being used as a framing schema. The inputs and outputs of the promoted operations are made explicit, which is useful for clients of the class. Our definition of method application [Lano and Haughton 1991] requires that the correct version of a method is used for a given object: that is, the version of the method defined in the class to which the object belongs. Attempting to perform *AngleQuad* on a quadrilateral which is not at least a parallelogram, for instance, is not legitimate.

9.3   Buttons Example

For this specification we assume the existence of the types *MouseLocation*, *Mouse-Click*, *Status* and *ACTION* as defined in section 2.3. The class of basic buttons is:

CLASS *Button*
OWNS
  loc : *MouseLocation*;
  click : *MouseClick*
OPERATIONS
  INIT : $\rightarrow$;
  PrimedMouseUp : $\rightarrow$;
  IgnoredMouseUp : $\rightarrow$;
  MouseUp : $\rightarrow$;
  MouseDown : $\rightarrow$;
  MouseLeave : $\rightarrow$;
  MouseEnter : $\rightarrow$
ACTIONS
  $INIT \ ==> \ loc' \ = \ Out \ \wedge \ click' \ = \ Up;$
  $PrimedMouseUp \ ==> \ click \ = \ Primed \ \wedge$
                $click' \ = \ Up;$
  $IgnoredMouseUp \ ==> \ click \ = \ Ignored \ \wedge$
                $click' \ = \ Up;$
  $MouseUp \ ==> \ PrimedMouseUp \ \vee \ IgnoredMouseUp;$
  $MouseDown \ ==> \ loc \ = \ In \ \wedge \ click' \ = \ Primed \quad \vee$
             $loc \ = \ Out \ \wedge \ click' \ = \ Ignored;$
  $MouseLeave \ ==> \ loc' \ = \ Out;$
  $MouseEnter \ ==> \ loc' \ = \ In$

END CLASS

ActionButtons produce *actions*:

CLASS *ActionButton*
   EXTENDS *Button*
FUNCTIONS
| *action* : $\mathbf{P}$ *ACTION*
OPERATIONS
 PrimedMouseUp : $\rightarrow$ ($\mathbf{P}$ *ACTION*);
 IgnoredMouseUp : $\rightarrow$ ($\mathbf{P}$ *ACTION*)
ACTIONS
 PrimedMouseUp out! ==> *out!* = *action* $\wedge$
                  Button.PrimedMouseUp;
 IgnoredMouseUp out! ==> *out!* = $\varnothing$ $\wedge$
                  Button.IgnoredMouseUp
END CLASS

This inheritance is a refinement, since no new constraints are added to the state of *Button*. The textual definition of other methods defined in *Button* remain unchanged, however the changed context of the class gives a modified definition to operations such as *MouseUp*, which now use the definition of methods given in *ActionButton*, and are functions on the extended state. *MouseUp* is defined as a disjoint union of relations, so preserves refinement [Lano and Haughton 1992].

CLASS *OnOffButton*
   EXTENDS *Button*
FUNCTIONS
| *initStatus* : *Status*
OWNS
 status : *Status*
OPERATIONS
 INIT : $\rightarrow$;
 PrimedMouseUp : $\rightarrow$
ACTIONS
 INIT ==> *status'* = *initStatus* $\wedge$
        Button.INIT ;
 PrimedMouseUp ==> *status'* $\in$ *Status* $\wedge$
        Button.PrimedMouseUp
END CLASS

Again, this class is a refinement of *Button*.

CLASS *ToggleButton*
   EXTENDS *OnOffButton*
INVARIANT
 initStatus = *Off*
OPERATIONS
 PrimedMouseUp : $\rightarrow$
ACTIONS
 PrimedMouseUp ==> *status'* $\neq$ *status* $\wedge$

$$OnOffButton.PrimedMouseUp$$
END CLASS

This class is a refinement of *OnOffButton*: the methods *INIT* and *PrimedMouseUp* are defined as procedural refinements of their previous versions.

CLASS *RadioButton*
    EXTENDS *OnOffButton*, *ActionButton*
INVARIANT
   $OnOffButton.loc = ActionButton.loc$
   $OnOffButton.click = ActionButton.click$
OPERATIONS
   $PrimedMouseUp : \rightarrow (\mathbf{P}\ ACTION);$
   $TurnOff : \rightarrow$
ACTIONS
   $PrimedMouseUp\ out!\ ==> \quad (status = Off \wedge out! = action \vee$
   $\qquad\qquad\qquad\qquad\qquad status = On \wedge out! = \emptyset) \wedge$
   $\qquad\qquad\qquad\qquad\qquad status' = On \quad \wedge$
   $\qquad\qquad\qquad\qquad\qquad ActionButton.PrimedMouseUp \wedge$
   $\qquad\qquad\qquad\qquad\qquad OnOffButton.PrimedMouseUp;$
   $IgnoredMouseUp\ out! \quad ==> \quad ActionButton.IgnoredMouseUp \wedge$
   $\qquad\qquad\qquad\qquad\qquad OnOffButton.IgnoredMouseUp;$
   $INIT \quad ==> \quad ActionButton.INIT \wedge$
   $\qquad\qquad\qquad OnOffButton.INIT\ ;$
   $TurnOff ==> status' = Off$
END CLASS

As with operations, attributes of the same name from distinct classes are qualified when necessary by prepending their names with the name of the appropriate class.

Our style is more explicit than Object-Z: we force the developer to name the version of an operation he is using in an inheriting class, and to make explicit the parameters for operations composed in this way. On the other hand, when changes are not made, nothing needs to be said. Our intention is to provide as much information about a class within its visible definition, without excessively cluttering this. This style is consistent with Z since Z requires the explicit listing of schemas when these are used as inherited states or operations.

10

ZEST

Elspeth Cusack and G. H. B. Rafsanjani[1]

10.1 Background

This chapter offers a snapshot of ZEST ('Z Extended with Structuring'), an ongoing research initiative in object oriented Z motivated by problems in distributed systems modelling: the International Organization for Standardization (ISO) Open Distributed Processing (ODP) project [ISO/IEC JTC1 SC21 WG7 N434 1991], [ISO/IEC JTC1 SC21 N6079 1991]. In particular, it is desired to clarify and express a series of object oriented modelling concepts being standardized for the specification of open distributed systems.

10.2 Concepts of ZEST

Objects are implemented entities with a persisting identity. An object is characterized by its behaviour and state ('methods' and 'variables' in object oriented programming language terminology). Each object is an implementation of an object specification. It is not necessary to consider objects separately from object specifications in this chapter — so we use the term object to mean an object specification.

The ideas introduced in this section are illustrated using fragments of the examples. They are based on a language-independent set-theoretic model developed in [Cusack and Lai 1991] which in turn was influenced by ideas from [Wegner and Zdonik 1988], [Wegner 1987b]. A sketch of the complete shapes example is given in section 10.3, and the buttons example is described in section 10.4.

10.2.1 Class Types

Types in conventional Z are sets of data values, primarily used for type checking. ZEST extends this system by adding *class types* — very similar to classes in Object-Z. A class type is a specification of the common behaviour pattern of a set of objects. All class types have a common syntactic form (or can be flattened into

---

[1] Communications Architectures Division, BT Application and Services Development, St. Vincent House, 1 Cutler Street, Ipswich, Suffolk, IP1 1UX.

this form, in the case of class types defined using incremental inheritance [Cusack 1991]). The generic syntax for a class type is as follows. The entry *Attributes* denotes an axiomatic definition. The other entries are usual schema boxes:

$$
\begin{array}{|l}
\hline
\_\,TYPE _____ \\
Attributes \\
State \\
InitialState \\
Operation_1 \\
\quad \vdots \\
Operation_n \\
\hline
\end{array}
$$

The axiomatic definition *Attributes* declares a number of *attributes* — values or objects which are fixed when an instance of the class type *TYPE* is created and do not change. At least one attribute is declared in each class type, corresponding to the persisting identity of each instance of the type. The schema *State* declares a number of *state variables* and the relationships which must hold between them. All attributes and state variables are declared to have a type in the extended type system. The schemas *Attributes* and *State* therefore determine a state space. The schema *InitialState* declares the valid initial states of a newly-created instance of the class type. If it is omitted, then any state may be an initial state.

Each schema *Operation_i* declares ways in which state or attribute values can be accessed by the environment. Each operation schema must include at least one of the following schema declarations:

- $\Xi Attributes$, where the operation permits the reading of an attribute value, or depends in some way on an attribute value

- $\Xi State$, where the operation permits some observation of the current state of the object, or depends in some way on the current state, but does not cause a state change

- $\Delta State$, where the operation leads to a change in the state of the object.

Note that $\Delta Attributes$ cannot be included because attributes are constants of each operation.

A class type *TYPE* can be used to form the set type $\mathbb{P}\,TYPE$ in the manner of conventional Z.

10.2.2 Instances Of Class Types

Each object is an *instance* of some class type. An instance of a class type is a partial specification formed from the class type by setting the values of the attributes declared in *Attributes*, choosing a valid initial state and giving actual names to the operations, their inputs and their outputs. Nothing else is added to the class type. Each object has a unique identity *object.name* as one of its attributes. We can therefore create actual names for the state and operation schemas, and inputs and outputs. In the example below, the actual names are based on the object identity

and the class type. The value $object.name * s_0$ in the schema below is the initial
state of the instance.

```
┌─ object.name * TYPE ─────────────────────────────────────────
│  ┌
│  │  object.name
│  │  attribute₂
│  │  ⋮
│  │  attribute_m
│  └
│  object.name * State
│  object.name * s₀
│  object.name * Operation₁
│  ⋮
│  object.name * Operation_n
└──────────────────────────────────────────────────────────────
```

We interpret the instance $object.name * TYPE$ as a partial specification of an
implemented object with identity $object.name$.

10.2.3 Subtyping

The set of instances of a class type t corresponds to the role of t as a template
or 'cookie-cutter'. There is however a second interesting set of objects associated
with each class type t. This set contains all these objects which satisfy t regarded
as a partial specification. We call the members of this set the *objects of type t*. We
declare an object of type t with identity $object.name$ by writing $object.name : t$.
The declaration $object.name : \mathbf{P}\, t$ is understood to mean that each member of
the set $object.name$ can be individually accessed by the environment through its
operations.

If each instance of a class type s is also an object of type t then we say that
s is a *subtype* of t (equivalently, t is a *supertype* of s). Any object of type t
must be an instance of some subtype s of t. This all implies that subtyping is
a preorder on class types (a preorder on a set is a relation which is reflexive and
transitive), indicating behavioural compatibility or type conformance. Subtyping
is the foundation of substitutability in object oriented modelling. If every object
of type t is an instance of some strict subtype of t, then we say that t is an *abstract
class type*.

If s is a subtype of t, the implication is that any instance $object.name * s$ of s can be
perceived as an object of type t. In the terminology of [Ehrich and Sernadas 1991]
it possesses a behavioural aspect $object.name * t$ of type t (a partial specification
of the object which suppresses all detail not defined in the class type t).

The statement $object.name : t$ declares an instance $object.name * s$ of some subtype
s of t.

In the examples, we infer subtype relationships from a stronger preorder on class
types called *extension*. The full definition of extension can be found in [Cusack
1991]. It depends on a precise comparison between the component schemas of the
class type and the extended type.

The *is-a* Relationship

The foundation of extension is the *is-a* relationship between class types. The full definition of *is-a* can be found in [Cusack 1991]. Loosely, we say that an object of type s *is-a(n)* (object of type) t if

- the state space of a class type s can be projected in a natural way into the state space of a class type t

- the projection take initial states to initial states.

If we let f denote the projection, then f is a coercion mapping which discards 'extra' components — that is, components defined by the state schema of s but not by the state schema of t. The *is-a* relationship suppresses details of operation schemas and therefore lets us make static comparisons between class types.

For example, with the basic type *Vector* and the following definitions of state schemas:

$$\begin{array}{|l}
\underline{\quad Quadrilateral\,}\underline{\qquad\qquad\qquad\qquad\qquad\qquad\qquad\qquad} \\
v1, v2, v3, v4 : Vector \\
position : Vector \\
\hline
v1 + v2 + v3 + v4 = \vec{0} \\
\hline
\end{array}$$

$$\begin{array}{|l}
\underline{\quad Parallelogram\,}\underline{\qquad\qquad\qquad\qquad\qquad\qquad\qquad\qquad} \\
Quadrilateral \\
\hline
v1 + v3 = \vec{0} \\
\hline
\end{array}$$

we find that an object of a class type with state schema *Parallelogram is-an* object of any class type with state schema *Quadrilateral*.

$$\begin{array}{|l}
\underline{\quad Rhombus\,}\underline{\qquad\qquad\qquad\qquad\qquad\qquad\qquad\qquad} \\
Parallelogram \\
\hline
\mid v1 \mid = \mid v2 \mid \\
\hline
\end{array}$$

Similarly, an object of a class type with state schema *Rhombus is-an* object of any class type with state schema *Parallelogram*.

The expressive power of *is-a* is limited. In order to consider the behaviour of objects representing different shapes — that is, how they respond to operations — we need to augment the definition of *is-a* to make it more powerful.

Extension

We say that a class type s *extends* a class type t if

- s *is-a* t

- to each operation P_i in t there corresponds a unique operation O_i in s such that (loosely) O_i 'projected' onto t using the *is-a* mapping has weaker pre-conditions and stronger post-conditions than P_i (essentially, we insist that O_i is a more deterministic version of P_i).

The definition permits s to have operations additional to those in t. Using the *is-a* mapping, the state of an object of type s can be regarded as having a value in the state space of t. The correspondence between operations P_i in t and O_i in s means that an object of type s can be regarded as responding to the operations defined in t. In this way, we argue that if s extends t, then s is a subtype of t.

For example, using the state schemas just introduced, the class type *PARALLEL-OGRAM* extends *QUADRILATERAL* :

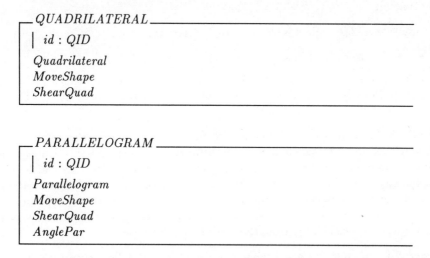

The operations *MoveShape* and *ShearQuad* include the declarations $\Delta\,Quadrilateral$ and $\Delta\,Parallelogram$ respectively. The operation *AnglePar* includes the declaration $\Xi\,Parallelogram$.

10.2.4   Incremental Inheritance

Incremental inheritance is the expression of a new class type as an incremental modification of an old one. There are several ways in which this can be done, with no *a priori* implication that the new class type is a subtype of the old one. Incremental inheritance lets us reuse class types we have already specified.

We use class type inclusion as an incremental inheritance technique. In the shapes example, we also use the incremental inheritance technique *derivation* whose definition (like that of extension) depends on a precise comparison between the component schemas of the parent class type and the derived type.

Class Type Inclusion

The simplest incremental inheritance technique is the inclusion of a class type already defined in a new one. We may include other definitions in the new class type, but we may not alter the included class type. If we restrict ourselves to adding only attributes and operations to the included type, but nothing else, then the new class type is an extension of the included one. For example, *QUADRILATERAL* is an extension of *QUADSHAPE*:

```
__QUADRILATERAL_____
  QUADSHAPE
  ShearQuad
```

There is nothing to prevent us including an existing class type definition in a new one, and adding more to it than attributes and operations. But in this case, there is no guarantee that the result is a subtype.

Derivation

We say that a class type s is *derived from* a class type t if

- s *is-a* t (as defined in section 10.2.3)

- to each operation P_i in t there corresponds a unique operation O_i in s such that (loosely) O_i is the restriction of P_i to the state space of s. (The full definition can be found in [Cusack 1991].)

The definition allows O_i to be undefined in s — for example, the result of non-trivially shearing a rectangle is never a rectangle. We interpret this to mean that the operation is simply not available on instances of s. In this case, although s is expressed in terms of t, instances of s are not of type t. Thus derivation is an incremental inheritance technique, since we express the derived type in terms of the parent type, the new attributes and state schema. The operations of the derived type are calculated from those of the parent type.

A derived type may be a subtype, but this does not follow automatically. We indicate that derivation is being used by employing the keywords *derived from*. This indicates that the operations defined in the derived type can be directly obtained from the parent class type.

```
__RHOMBUS_____
 | id : QID
  Rhombus
  derived from PARALLELSHAPE
```

10.2.5   Composition

The attributes and state variables of a class type may themselves be declared in terms of existing of class types — in other words, they may themselves be objects or sets of objects, rather than values in conventional Z types. Such class types are described as *composite*. We have identified and are currently researching two distinct forms of composition — we call them *product composition* and *meta composition* [Rafsanjani 1992]. A composite class type is a product or meta composition of a particular set of class types already defined. A particular class type may therefore simultaneously be a product composition of one set of class types and a meta composition of a second set. Neither form of composition gives details of how component objects are combined — that depends on the precise specification of the composite class type. The examples in this chapter use meta composition only.

Meta Composition

A composite class type may possess state variables declared in terms of existing class types. For the purposes of this chapter, this means that the class type has some 'component objects' which are 'object-valued state variables'. In this case, we say that the composite class type is a meta composition of the class types used in the declarations of the objects or sets of objects which are state variables. A meta composition may contain operations which change object-valued state variables to other objects of the declared type.

If a state variable is a set of objects, then there may be operations in the meta composition which alter its membership. For example, the class type *DRAW-INGSYSTEM* is a meta composition of *QUADSHAPE*:

```
┌─ DRAWINGSYSTEM ─────────────────────────────────────
│  ┌─ DrawingSystem ──────────────────────────
│  │  screen : P QUADSHAPE
│  ├──────────────────────────────────────────────
│  AddShape
│  DeleteShape
└──────────────────────────────────────────────────
```

10.3 The Shapes Example

The first part of the problem is to classify the possible class types of shape objects in a drawing system. We do this by defining a hierarchy of class types ordered by the subtype relation (see figure 10.1). In order to achieve such a hierarchy, we introduce two abstract class types. Incremental inheritance is used where appropriate. This leads to efficient specification, reusing what we have already. We assume that the types *QID*, *Vector*, *Shear*, *Scalar* and *Angle*, and conventional operations on them, are given.

We begin with the abstract class type *QUADSHAPE*. We choose to declare the edges and position as state variables rather than as attributes because there is no requirement that they remain fixed in any object. *QUADSHAPE* is the root of our class type hierarchy. Its introduction simplifies the eventual specification of the drawing system, as all shapes are of class type *QUADSHAPE*:

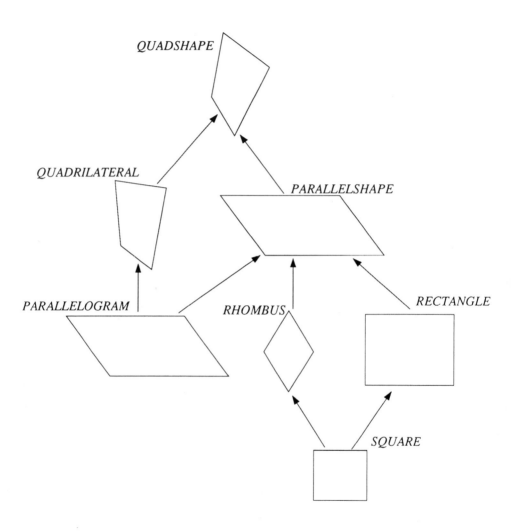

Figure 10.1: The shapes hierarchy of class types ordered by the subtype relation

```
┌─ QUADSHAPE ─────────────────────────────────────────────
│ id : QID
│ ┌─ Quadrilateral ──────────────────────────────────────
│ │ v1, v2, v3, v4 : Vector
│ │ position : Vector
│ ├──────────────────────────────────────────────────────
│ │ v1 + v2 + v3 + v4 = 0⃗
│ └──────────────────────────────────────────────────────
│ ┌─ MoveShape ──────────────────────────────────────────
│ │ ΔQuadrilateral
│ │ move? : Vector
│ ├──────────────────────────────────────────────────────
│ │ position' = position + move?
│ │ ∀ i : {1, 2, 3, 4} • vi' = vi
│ └──────────────────────────────────────────────────────
└──────────────────────────────────────────────────────────
```

We define two immediate subtypes. The first of these, *PARALLELSHAPE*, is again an abstract class type.

```
┌─ PARALLELSHAPE ─────────────────────────────────────────
│ id : QID
│ ┌─ Parallelogram ──────────────────────────────────────
│ │ Quadrilateral
│ ├──────────────────────────────────────────────────────
│ │ v1 + v3 = 0⃗
│ └──────────────────────────────────────────────────────
│ derived from QUADSHAPE
│ ┌─ AnglePar ───────────────────────────────────────────
│ │ ΞParallelogram
│ │ a! : Angle
│ ├──────────────────────────────────────────────────────
│ │ (calculation of a! using cos⁻¹ omitted)
│ └──────────────────────────────────────────────────────
└──────────────────────────────────────────────────────────
```

and

```
┌─ QUADRILATERAL ─────────────────────────────────────────
│ QUADSHAPE
│ ┌─ ShearQuad ──────────────────────────────────────────
│ │ ΔQuadrilateral
│ │ s? : Scalar
│ ├──────────────────────────────────────────────────────
│ │ (calculation of vi' and position' omitted)
│ └──────────────────────────────────────────────────────
└──────────────────────────────────────────────────────────
```

Parallelograms are of class type *PARALLELOGRAM*, a subtype of *QUADRILAT-ERAL*. The definition re-uses the state schema *Parallelogram* defined in *PARALLELSHAPE* — we avoid clutter by simply giving the name rather than repeating the full definition.

```
┌─ PARALLELOGRAM ────────────────────────────
│ id : QID
│
│ Parallelogram
│ derived from QUADRILATERAL
│ derived from PARALLELSHAPE
└────────────────────────────────────────────
```

PARALLELOGRAM can be proved to extend both *QUADRILATERAL* and *PARALLELSHAPE*, and so is a subtype of both of these class types.

We specify the class type *RHOMBUS* as a derivation of *PARALLELSHAPE*:

```
┌─ RHOMBUS ──────────────────────────────────
│ id : QID
│
│ ┌─ Rhombus ────────────────────────────────
│ │ Parallelogram
│ │
│ │ | v1 |=| v2 |
│ └──────────────────────────────────────────
│ derived from PARALLELSHAPE
└────────────────────────────────────────────
```

Similarly, we specify the class type *RECTANGLE*:

```
┌─ RECTANGLE ────────────────────────────────
│ id : QID
│
│ ┌─ Rectangle ──────────────────────────────
│ │ Parallelogram
│ │
│ │ v1.v2 = 0
│ └──────────────────────────────────────────
│ derived from PARALLELSHAPE
└────────────────────────────────────────────
```

RHOMBUS and *RECTANGLE* are both subtypes of *PARALLELSHAPE*. We could derive a specification of *RHOMBUS* with the same semantics from *QUADRILATERAL*, as the construction would prohibit the shear operation. But as we have the definition of *PARALLELSHAPE* available, there is no reason to reuse *QUADRILATERAL*. It also seems more sensible, where possible, to derive a class type from a supertype.

To specify *SQUARE*, we use the usual Z schema calculus notation to define *Square* = *Rhombus* ∧ *Rectangle*:

```
┌─ SQUARE ───────────────────────────────────
│ id : QID
│
│ Square
│ derived from RHOMBUS
└────────────────────────────────────────────
```

Notice that *SQUARE* could equally well have been defined from *RECTANGLE*. However defined, *SQUARE* is a subtype of both *RHOMBUS* and *RECTANGLE*.

Class type *DRAWINGSYSTEM* is a meta composition of class type *QUADSHAPE*. We assume that *DSID* is a given Z type. The specification describes precisely the interface offered to the user by the drawing system. The user may add new objects to the screen or delete those already there. Each new object is an instance of some subtype of *QUADSHAPE*, and so is of type *QUADSHAPE*. The user may move, shear or query the angle of displayed shape objects directly, according to the class types of which they are instances. The choice of which object to manipulate is the user's. The user invokes the required operation on the object and leaves the others unchanged.

DRAWINGSYSTEM

$id : DSID$

> **DrawingSystem**
> $screen : \mathbb{P}\ QUADSHAPE$

> **Init**
> $screen = \varnothing$

> **AddShape**
> $\Delta DrawingSystem$
> $q? : QUADSHAPE$
>
> $q? \notin screen$
> $screen' = screen \cup \{q?\}$

> **DeleteShape**
> $\Delta DrawingSystem$
> $q? : QUADSHAPE$
>
> $q? \in screen$
> $screen' = screen \setminus \{q?\}$

10.4   The Buttons Example

The common features of all the various button objects are specified in the class type *BUTTON*. We assume the basic Z types *MouseLocation* and *MouseClick* are given, and introduce a third basic type *BID*. We require *BUTTON* to be an abstract class type :

```
┌─ BUTTON ──────────────────────────────────────────────
│  id : BID
│
│  ┌─ Button ──────────────────────────────────────────
│  │  loc : MouseLocation
│  │  click : MouseClick
│  └──────────────────────────────────────────────────
│
│  ┌─ Init ────────────────────────────────────────────
│  │  Button
│  │ ─────────────────────────────────────
│  │  loc = Out
│  │  click = Up
│  └──────────────────────────────────────────────────
│
│  ┌─ MouseLeave ──────────────────────────────────────
│  │  ΔButton
│  │ ─────────────────────────────────────
│  │  loc' = Out
│  │  click' = click
│  └──────────────────────────────────────────────────
│
│  ┌─ MouseEnter ──────────────────────────────────────
│  │  ΔButton
│  │ ─────────────────────────────────────
│  │  loc' = In
│  │  click' = click
│  └──────────────────────────────────────────────────
│
│  ┌─ MouseDown ───────────────────────────────────────
│  │  ΔButton
│  │ ─────────────────────────────────────
│  │  loc' = loc
│  │  ((loc = In ∧ click' = Primed)
│  │  ∨     (loc = Out ∧ click' = Ignored))
│  └──────────────────────────────────────────────────
└───────────────────────────────────────────────────────
```

The class type *ACTIONBUTTON* makes use of the given type *Action* (written in lower case in order to avoid confusion with our class type notation). *ACTION-BUTTON* is an extension of *BUTTON*. The set *action* is declared as an attribute because it is fixed for each object of type *ACTIONBUTTON*.

```
┌─ ACTIONBUTTON ────────────────────────────────────────
│  action : P Action
│  BUTTON
│
│  ┌─ MouseUp ─────────────────────────────────────────
│  │  ΔButton
│  │  act! : P Action
│  │ ─────────────────────────────────────
│  │  ((click = Ignored ∧ act! = ∅)
│  │  ∨     (click = Primed ∧ act! = action))
│  │  loc' = loc
│  │  click' = Up
│  └──────────────────────────────────────────────────
└───────────────────────────────────────────────────────
```

The abstract class type *ONOFFBUTTON* is also an extension of *BUTTON*. We assume the type *Status* is given.

```
┌─ ONOFFBUTTON ──────────────────────────────────────────
│ │ id : BID
│
│ ┌─ OnOffButton ────────────────────────────────────
│ │ Button
│ │ status : Status
│ └──────────────────────────────────────────────────
│
│ ┌─ Init ───────────────────────────────────────────
│ │ OnOffButton
│ ├──────────────────────────────────────────────────
│ │ loc = Out
│ │ click = Up
│ └──────────────────────────────────────────────────
│
│ ┌─ MouseLeave ─────────────────────────────────────
│ │ Δ OnOffButton
│ ├──────────────────────────────────────────────────
│ │ loc' = Out
│ │ click' = click
│ │ status' = status
│ └──────────────────────────────────────────────────
│
│ ┌─ MouseEnter ─────────────────────────────────────
│ │ Δ OnOffButton
│ ├──────────────────────────────────────────────────
│ │ loc' = In
│ │ click' = click
│ │ status' = status
│ └──────────────────────────────────────────────────
│
│ ┌─ MouseDown ──────────────────────────────────────
│ │ Δ OnOffButton
│ ├──────────────────────────────────────────────────
│ │ loc' = loc
│ │ ((loc = In ∧ click' = Primed)
│ │ ∨    (loc = Out ∧ click' = Ignored))
│ │ status' = status
│ └──────────────────────────────────────────────────
└────────────────────────────────────────────────────────
```

We might have chosen a shorter definition of *ONOFFBUTTON* as a derived type of *BUTTON*. However, this would have left undefined the effect of each operation on the variable *status*, which is not what we require.

The class type *TOGGLEBUTTON* is defined by adding the operation *MouseUpToggle* to *ONOFFBUTTON*. *TOGGLEBUTTON* is thus easily seen to be an extension of *ONOFFBUTTON*.

```
┌─ TOGGLEBUTTON ──────────────────────────────────
│ ONOFFBUTTON
│
│ ┌─ MouseUpToggle ────────────────────────────────
│ │ Δ OnOffButton
│ ├─────────────────────────────────────────────────
│ │ loc′ = loc
│ │ click′ = Up
│ │ ((click = Primed ∧ status′ ≠ status)
│ │ ∨ (click = Ignored ∧ status′ = status))
│ └─────────────────────────────────────────────────
└──────────────────────────────────────────────────
```

RADIOBUTTON extends both *ACTIONBUTTON* and *ONOFFBUTTON*.

```
┌─ RADIOBUTTON ───────────────────────────────────
│ action : P Action
│ ONOFFBUTTON
│
│ ┌─ MouseUpRadio ─────────────────────────────────
│ │ Δ OnOffButton
│ ├─────────────────────────────────────────────────
│ │ loc′ = loc
│ │ click′ = Up
│ │ (    (click = Ignored ∧ status′ = status ∧ act! = ∅)
│ │ ∨    (click = Primed ∧
│ │      (    status = Off ∧ act! = action
│ │      ∨    status = On ∧ act! = ∅)
│ │      ∧status′ = On))
│ └─────────────────────────────────────────────────
│
│ ┌─ TurnOff ──────────────────────────────────────
│ │ Δ OnOffButton
│ ├─────────────────────────────────────────────────
│ │ loc′ = loc
│ │ click′ = click
│ │ status = On
│ │ status′ = Off
│ └─────────────────────────────────────────────────
└──────────────────────────────────────────────────
```

Instantiation

The creation of new buttons with a given value of *action* and a particular initial value *status* would need to be specified as an operation of a 'button creator' object. Ideas on how this could be done can be found in [Cusack 1992].

Acknowledgement

We are grateful to Steve Rudkin and Jeremy Wilson for their contributions to ZEST, and to Sukhvinder Aujla for his helpful comments as this chapter was drafted.

11

Specification in Fresco

Alan Wills[1]

11.1 The Fresco method

Fresco [Wills 1991] is a programming environment which provides for the rigorous development of object-oriented software from specifications. Specifications are incorporated into the software in the form of abstract classes; and the specification elements of the language can also be used in concrete classes to document the implementations and their development in a style similar to that of [Morgan 1990]. It is interesting to contrast Fresco with object-oriented styles of specification: firstly because it is based on VDM [Jones 1986], rather than Z; and secondly because of its emphasis on specifying program modules, rather than modularizing specifications.

The first difference has little impact on any comparison of style with, say, Object Z; but the second makes a profound difference to our approach to the example.

In Fresco, a class can describe a specification or an implementation, or, most commonly, a mixture of the two — in which case, the programmer ought to verify that the implementation meets the specification. The implementation is described with programming language code, and the specification with class variables (like Object Z's state schema variables), invariants, and operation specifications. The Fresco browser provides a Smalltalk-like interface to the heirarchy of definitions, but on paper we use this notation:

ClassName
visible operation signatures • operation specifications • invariants
private model variables or private implementation

Any part may be omitted, and the same class may be defined in several different boxes: any implementation must conform to the specifications in all the boxes (and it is up to the designer not to specify conflicting requirements).

---

[1] University of Manchester, Department of Computer Science, Manchester, M13 9PL.

Operations are specified by 'opspecs', pre-postcondition pairs:

$$[\text{ pre}(\textit{ before }) :- \text{post}(\odot \textit{before, after })] \text{ result}:= \text{op}(\text{parms})$$

The specification states that if the precondition is satisfied by the prior state, then the operation terminates with all values well-defined and conforming to their invariants, and the postcondition relates the before (marked by $\odot$) and after states. (We discuss framing in due course.) Any number of opspecs may apply to the same operation, whose implementation must satisfy all of them; we encode this interpretation in the Fresco inference rule:

$$\frac{\begin{array}{c} [\text{pre1} :- \text{post1}] \text{ op} \\ [\text{pre2} :- \text{post2}] \text{ op} \end{array}}{[\text{ pre1} \lor \text{pre2} :- (\odot\text{pre1} \Rightarrow \text{post1}) \land (\odot\text{pre2} \Rightarrow \text{post2})] \text{ op}}$$

which is related to the strengthening rule

$$\frac{\begin{array}{c} \text{pre} \vdash \text{pre1} \\ \text{post1} \vdash \text{post} \\ [\text{pre1} :- \text{post1}] \text{ s} \end{array}}{[\text{pre} :- \text{post}] \text{ s}}$$

The benefits of this advance from traditional VDM include:

- as with Z schemata different aspects of an operation (e.g. success and failure behaviour) can be described separately;

- we can compose specifications imposed on an operation from one or more supertype(s) and extended within a subclass;

- we can compose specifications from older and newer versions of published software components, to ensure compatibility.

There are in effect two hierarchies in a Fresco system: the 'class hierarchy' of implementations; and the 'type hierarchy' of type conformance. The favoured form of inheritance combines the two in 'conformant inheritance', in which the subclass also happens to implement a subtype. ([Meyer 1988] puts good arguments for this preference.) In another variation, a subclass may specify and implement a subrange of the supertype, in which the preconditions of some of the supertype's operations are strengthened, but the postconditions remain the same (or stronger, which is permitted for conformance). This is also generally frowned upon in Fresco, for the following reasons.

In Fresco, a great deal of emphasis is lain on conformance as the key to polymorphism. For example, this FigureManipulator class deals successfully with any Figure:

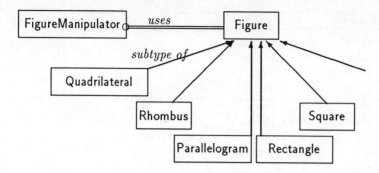

The purpose of Figure is to specify what FigureManipulator can manipulate. It is dependent upon Figure, in the sense that if Figure were altered, FigureManipulator would have to be examined, possibly altered too, and in any case reverified. These dependency diagrams are a powerful tool in software maintenance. However, FigureManipulator is not dependent upon all the subtypes of Figure: provided they really are subtypes, they all behave at least in the way Figure stipulates (as well as doing more that FigureManipulator isn't interested in). Furthermore, we could add new subtypes of Figure, and FigureManipulator would deal with them just as well, without any need for reverification (of the latter; obviously we need to verify that the new type really is a subtype of Figure, but this is a cheaper proposition than going around all the dependents of Figure, many of which may be unknown to its author).

Clearly a subrange type is just as bad as a nonconformant type from this point of view. If we invent a subrange of Figure, there is no guarantee that FigureManipulator (or any of its other dependents) work with the new type, and we have to go around reverifying them. And if FigureManipulator was prepared to work with some subrange, why did its author stipulate Figure in the first place?

11.2   Figures

Whilst a static Square is clearly substitutable where a static Quadrilateral value is required, a mutable Square-representing object is not substitutable for a Quadrilateral-representing object, because the Square-object cannot, amongst other things, be sheared. So whilst in the world of static values, SVSquare is a subtype of SVQuadrilateral, the same is not true in the world of mutable objects. Indeed, one might consider the reverse to be the case, since, given an object capable of representing quadrilaterals, one can certainly use it to represent any square; but it is not quite true, because a function expecting a Square might be given a Quadrilateral not initialized to a square.

We therefore conclude that Quadrilaterals and Squares are not true subtypes of each other; but seek a common supertype, which we call Figure, which can be used by their common dependents as a specification of those features they depend upon:

Figure
move:　　　　　　(Vector)
rotate:　　　　　　(Angle)
position:　　　　　Vector
v1,v2,v3,v4:　　　Vector
p1, p2, p3, p4:　　Point
set-p1, ... set-p4: (Vector)
• [:– position = ⊙position + v] move(v)
• [:– ...*omitted...*] rotate(ω)
• v1 + v2 + v3 + v4 = 0
// p1...p4 are redundant ...
• p1=position ∧ p2=p1+v1 ∧ p3=p2+v2 ∧ p4=p3+v3
• [:– p1 = x] set-p1(x) //etc

A Figure can be moved and rotated, and its position and edges can be read. We also know that we can set a vertex however we like: but notice there's nothing said about what happens to the other vertices in the process. An invariant of the edges is stated, together with an invariant relating the two equally convenient ways of describing the Figure, by its edges and its vertices.

None of the figures in our system are merely Figures, but also have their own characteristics. A Quadrilateral can be sheared, and its vertices can be set individually:

Quadrilateral
Figure +::
shear:　　(Shear)
• [:– ...*omitted...*] shear(s)
• [:– p3 = ⊙p3 ∧ p4 = ⊙p4] set-p1(x)
• [:– p1 = ⊙p1 ∧ p4 = ⊙p4] set-p2(x) //etc

A Square has an extra invariant, determining what happens in set-p_i:

Square
Figure +::
• v1+v3=0 ∧ |v1|=|v2| ∧ v1⊥v2

Clearly if **Square** had been derived from **Quadrilateral**, the result would be unimplementable, as **Square**'s invariant and the postconditions imposed by **Quadrilateral** could not be satisfied simultaneously; whereas there is no difficulty in satisfying both **Square** and **Figure**.

11.3   Drawing System

A DrawingSystem contains a set of Figures:

DrawingSystem		
drawing:	IdSet (Figure)	// 'Id' - one of each *object*
add:	(Figure)	
delete:	(Figure)	
• [	:– drawing = ⊙drawing ∪ {f}] add(f)	
• [f ∈ drawing	:– drawing = ⊙drawing – {f}] delete(f)	
update:	(Figure)	
• [fx ∈ drawing ∧ fx≠f :– fx = ⊙fx] update(f)		

update's declaration appears in the 'private' partition of the box, indicating that it is not intended as part of the interface, but is purely a device of the model. Its purpose is to characterize what is common to all operations which apply only to one figure within the drawing, and we use it in promoted form inside the opspecs of move and rotate:

DrawingSystem	
move:	(Figure, Vector)
rotate:	(Figure, Angle)
• [f ∈ drawing :– ⟦f.move(v)⟧ ∧ ⟦update(f)⟧] move (f,v)	
• [f ∈ drawing :– ⟦f.rotate(a)⟧ ∧ ⟦update(f)⟧] rotate (f,a)	

(This box's contents can be considered to be merged with all others headed DrawingSystem.)

The ⟦...⟧ notation 'promotes' an operation to become part of the specification of another: move(f,v) applied to any DrawingSystem has, if f ∈ drawing is true beforehand, an effect equivalent to applying Figure::move(v) to f, and also of applying update(f) in the local context. More precisely, there is an inference rule:

$$\frac{[\ \text{pre} :- \llbracket w:= x.op(p) \rrbracket\ ]\ s \qquad [\ z{:}T \wedge \text{pre-op}(q,v) :- \text{post-op}\ (q,\ \odot z.v,\ z.v,\ r)\ ]\ r := z.op(q)}{[\ \text{pre} \wedge x{:}T \wedge \text{pre-op}(p,\ x.v) :- \text{post-op}(p,\ \odot x.v,\ x.v,\ w)\ ]\ s}$$

Two asides on this rule:

- The second hypothesis is in the form typical of opspecs which have been extracted from the context of their class, in this case T, and have had the operand (z) and typing precondition (z:T) made explicit.

- Whilst there are rules which can be used to pull apart a conjunction of terms within an opspec, there is no rule which deals with a postcondition term ¬⟦...⟧: so there's no point in designers trying to write negative promotions. This is essential, because we can never guarantee to have seen all the rules which might apply to a particular operation, and so should not be able to say what it might mean definitely not to comply with its spec.

We should like to be able to apply shear to those figures in the drawing which happen to be Quadrilaterals:

DrawingSystem
shear: (Figure, Shear)
• [f ∈ drawing :– ⟦f.shear(s)⟧ ∧ ⟦update(f)⟧] shear (f,s)

Looking for ways of applying the expansion rule above, we have no success taking T to be **Figure**, as there is no op in **Figure** called **shear** (or, equivalently, the precondition of **Figure::shear** is false); but we can succeed with **Quadrilateral**: so that the conclusion is that we can prove that if we try to shear an instance of the latter, we can be certain of the result; whilst we have proved nothing about what might happen if we try to shear one of the other figures in the drawing.

11.4   Buttons

11.4.1   Button ancestor class

We describe the four client-accessible operations with the help of two model variables:

Button
mouseUp: ()
mouseDown: ()
mouseEnter: ()
mouseLeave: ()
loc: MouseLocation
click: MouseClick
• [:– loc = OUT] mouseLeave ()
• [:– loc = IN] mouseEnter ()
• [:– click = UP] mouseUp ()
• [loc = IN :– click = PRIMED] mouseDown ()
• [loc = OUT :– click = IGNORED] mouseDown()

A model initialization helps to describe creation operations:

Button
init ()
• [:– loc = OUT ∧ click = UP] init ()

11.4.2   OnOffButton and framing

An On-Off Button is a Button which has a status which is changed only by mouseUp, but not if the mouse has not been inside the button:

OnOffButton
Button +::
status: Status
• [click ≠ PRIMED :– status = ⊙status] mouseUp

This rather highlights the omission we have made so far, of any description of the frames of the operations. Fresco regards these as postconditions, so we can write:

OnOffButton
[:– Δ\{click, status\}] mouseUp

The Δ-term says that all other variables known in this context are unaffected by this operation. More than one Δ-term applying to the same operation would reduce the frame, unless disjoint preconditions were used: this is necessary to preserve any individual Δ-opspec's guarantee that the operation does not disturb the excluded variables. The unfortunate consequence is that we have to gather all the framing information about an operation into one place in each class, which works against the aim of distributing different aspects of behaviour amongst different opspecs. However, since a Δ-term only applies to the current context, we can extend the set to include new model components in a subtype: so, for example, OnOffButton::mouseUp has been extended to alter **status**.

Framing specifications are generally omitted here, for brevity.

11.4.3   ToggleButton and instance-creation

A ToggleButton is an OnOffButton always switched by mouseUp:

ToggleButton
OnOffButton +::
• [click = PRIMED :- status $\neq$ $\odot$status] mouseUp

Instances of a class are constructed with functions named after the class. Let's describe one creation function, with no parameters. Creation functions are not part of the behaviour exhibited by any instance, and hence not part of the type definition; but it's convenient to write their definitions in with the class all the same, since a class is not merely a mathematical object, but also a package of software engineering effort:

ToggleButton
• [:– b.status = OFF $\wedge$ [[b.init()]]] b:= ToggleButton()

11.4.4   ActionButton and callback

An Action Button applies an operation to a recipient specified by the client, using a set of actions and its own identity as parameters. We avoid difficulties of introducing higher-order functions by stipulating a single operation, **happen**, to signal the action:

ActionButton
Button +::   ActionButton: (Set (Action), MouseVictim) ActionButton
action: Set (Action)   recipient: MouseVictim   • [:– ab .action = what ∧ &ab .recipient = &toWhom]   ab:= ActionButton (what, toWhom)   • [click = PRIMED :– ⟦recipient.happen(action, self)⟧] mouseUp()   • [click ≠ PRIMED :– recipient = ⊙recipient] mouseUp ()

Notice that we explicitly say that recipient and toWhom must be *identical*.

Anything which is to be a recipient of ActionButton has to have a happen operation, but we don't care how it deals with it; that is, it must be a subtype of MouseVictim:

MouseVictim
happen: (Set(Action), Object)   • [true :–] happen (x,y)

In Fresco (as in VDM), satisfying a precondition guarantees well-behaved termination of an operation, even if we don't know what the results are: so it is always be permissible to call happen. ActionButton needs this because we don't know anything else about the recipient.

11.4.5   RadioButton — strict conformance

A RadioButton is an OnOffButton and also a ConditionalActionButton, together with a turn-off operation:

RadioButton
OnOffButton +::   ConditionalActionButton +::   turnOff: ()
• [click = PRIMED :– status = ON] mouseUp   • [:– status = OFF] turnOff ()

A ConditionalActionButton differs from an ActionButton, in that its response to mouseUp depends on status; whereas one of the opspecs of ActionButton guarantees to clients that mouseUp with click = PRIMED always results in recipient.happen. ConditionalActionButton's instances are therefore not substitutable for those of ActionButton, and so neither it nor RadioButton are subtypes of ActionButton.

ConditionalActionButton
Button +::
action: Set (Action) recipient: MouseVictim status: Status • [click = PRIMED ∧ status = OFF :– [[recipient.happen(action, self)]]] mouseUp() • [click ∧ PRIMED :– recipient = ⊙recipient] mouseUp ()

status is not set by anything in ConditionalActionButton: it is identified with the status mentioned in OnOffButton.

11.5   Fresco summary

The specification component of Fresco is intended to facilitate the description of re-usable software components, and, just as in many OO programming languages, the notion of distinct objects is generally implicit, and explicitly dealt with only where necessary. Implementation and specification descriptions are integrated into one notation, though we have seen examples here only of the specification component (clothed in a concrete syntax chosen for convenience: there are variants of Fresco derived from C++ and Smalltalk, which each use syntax closer to their origins). The language of class descriptions is intended to permit different aspects of the behaviour and relationships of classes to be described separately. The same mechanism permits constraints to be placed on a class and its operations by one or more ancestors; and a promotion mechanism permits specifications of different operations to be combined. Conformance is based on the substitutability of mutable objects, rather than static values: subclasses obey all the laws of their ancestors.

A

Z and HOOD

HOOD — Hierarchical Object Oriented Design — is the approved European Space Agency design method for Ada. It is not actually object oriented, since it has no idea of classes or inheritance; it is object *based* (as is Ada). The hierarchical design approach consists of decomposing a parent object into several child objects which act together to provide the functionality of the parent.

In conventional HOOD, the more 'formal' parts of the specification are achieved by using Ada as a program description language. [Giovanni and Iachini 1990] describe a way to use Z to specify the HOOD objects. A parent object is specified abstractly (a WHAT specification), using Z to specify an abstract state and abstract operations. The child objects, identified by the HOOD design process, are specified abstractly (as a WHAT specification, or as a WHAT-WITH specification for objects that use other objects). The parent object is then re-specified, more concretely in terms of these child objects (a HOW specification), by defining how its abstract state and operations are built from its children and their operations.

The approach differs from plain Z in two ways:

1. It uses HOOD constructs to limit the scope of the Z definitions. For example, child operation definitions are not visible outside the parent.

2. It extends Z's dot notation to refer to particular objects' operations.

As a trivial example (not using the WHAT-WITH specifications), consider an abstract parent specification that has an (internal) state specified by *State* and a series of available operations *Op1*, ... Its HOOD+Z specification would look something like:

WHAT Parent ::=

$$
\begin{array}{l}
\text{\underline{\quad Parent \rule{0pt}{0pt}}} \\
\quad State \\
\hline
\end{array}
$$

$$
\begin{array}{l}
\text{\underline{\quad Op1 \rule{0pt}{0pt}}} \\
\quad \Delta Parent \\
\hline
\quad pred \\
\end{array}
$$

(other operations)

END Parent

The HOOD process might then decompose the parent into various child objects, each with a specification looking like:

*WHAT Child*1 ::=

```
┌─ Child1 ──────────────────────────────────
│ state
│
│
└──────────────────────────────────────────
```

```
┌─ Op1 ─────────────────────────────────────
│ Δ Child1
│ ────────────
│ pred
│
└──────────────────────────────────────────
```

(other operations)

*END Child*1

The parent's concrete specification, in terms of its children, might then look like:

HOW Parent ::=

```
┌─ Parent ──────────────────────────────────
│ Child1
│ Child2
│ . . .
│
└──────────────────────────────────────────
```

$Op1 == Child1.Op1$
$Op2 == Child2.Op1$
$Op3 == Child2.Op2$

. . .

END Parent

These two extensions give Z a full object-based capability: local scope and the ability to apply operations to objects. [Iachini 1991] describes a proposed notation to allow operation schemas to be iterated (giving something analogous to a 'while loop'), since such constructs can occur in the internals of object specifications.

HOOD also supports concurrency (in the Ada style) — the authors want to extend their Z work to cover this aspect, too. If they are successful, this appears to be a promising approach to 'firming up' HOOD and Ada designs.

B

Bibliography

[Alencar and Goguen 1991]
>   Antonio J. Alencar and Joseph A. Goguen. OOZE: An Object Oriented Z
>   Environment. In [America 1991], pages 180–199.

[America 1991]
>   Pierre America, editor. *ECOOP'91: European Conference on Object-
>   Oriented Programming*, volume 512 of *Lecture Notes in Computer Science*.
>   Springer Verlag, 1991.

[Barden *et al.* 1992]
>   Rosalind Barden, Susan Stepney, and David Cooper. The use of Z. In
>   [Nicholls 1992].

[Bjørner *et al.* 1990]
>   Dines Bjørner, C. A. R. Hoare, and H. Langmaack, editors. *VDM'90: VDM
>   and Z — Formal Methods in Software Development, Kiel*, volume 428 of
>   *Lecture Notes in Computer Science*. Springer Verlag, 1990.

[Booch 1991]
>   Grady Booch. *Object Oriented Design with Applications*. Benjamin-
>   Cummings, 1991.

[Brownbridge 1990]
>   David Brownbridge. Using Z to develop a CASE toolset. In [Nicholls 1990],
>   pages 142–149.

[Burstall and Goguen 1980]
>   R. M. Burstall and Joseph A. Goguen. The semantics of Clear, a specifi-
>   cation language. In Dines Bjørner, editor, *Abstract Software Specifications*,
>   volume 86 of *Lecture Notes in Computer Science*, pages 292–332. Springer
>   Verlag, 1980.

[Carrington *et al.* 1990]
>   David A. Carrington, David Duke, Roger Duke, Paul King, Gordon A.
>   Rose, and Graeme Smith. Object-Z: An object-oriented extension to Z.
>   In S. Vuong, editor, *Formal Description Techniques II, FORTE'89*, pages
>   281–296. North Holland, 1990.

[Carrington 1992]
>   David A. Carrington. ZOOM workshop report. In [Nicholls 1992].

140   *Bibliography*

[Cox 1986]
Brad J. Cox. *Object Oriented Programming — An Evolutionary Approach.* Addison-Wesley, 1986.

[Cusack and Lai 1991]
Elspeth Cusack and Mike Lai. Object oriented specification in LOTOS and Z. In J. W. de Bakker, W. P. de Roever, and G. Rozenberg, editors, *Foundations of Object Oriented Languages, Proceedings of the REX School/Workshop May/June 1990*, number 489 in Lecture Notes in Computer Science. Springer Verlag, 1991.

[Cusack 1991]
Elspeth Cusack. Inheritance in object oriented Z. In [America 1991], pages 167–179.

[Cusack 1992]
Elspeth Cusack. Object oriented modelling in Z. In J. de Meer, editor, *International Workshop on ODP, October 1991.* North Holland, 1992.

[Duke and Duke 1990]
David Duke and Roger Duke. Towards a semantics for Object-Z. In [Bjørner *et al.* 1990], pages 244–261.

[Duke *et al.* 1991]
Roger Duke, Paul King, Gordon A. Rose, and Graeme Smith. The Object-Z specification language version 1. Technical Report 91-1, Software Verification Research Centre, Department of Computer Science, University of Queensland, May 1991.

[Ehrich and Sernadas 1991]
H.-D. Ehrich and A. Sernadas. Fundamental object concepts and constructions. Report 91-03, Technische Universität Braunschweig, 1991.

[Enderton 1977]
H. B. Enderton. *Elements of Set Theory.* Academic Press, 1977.

[Flynn *et al.* 1990]
Mike Flynn, Tim Hoverd, and David Brazier. Formaliser — an interactive support tool for Z. In [Nicholls 1990], pages 128–141.

[Giovanni and Iachini 1990]
R. Di Giovanni and P. Luigi Iachini. HOOD and Z for the development of complex systems. In [Bjørner *et al.* 1990], pages 262–289.

[Goguen *et al.* 1992a]
Joseph A. Goguen, Andrew Stevens, Hendrik Hilberdink, and Keith Hobley. 2OBJ, a metalogical framework based on equational logic. *Transactions of the Royal Society, Series A*, 1992. to appear.

[Goguen *et al.* 1992b]
Joseph A. Goguen, Timothy Winkler, José Meseguer, Kokichi Futatsugi, and Jean-Pierre Jouannaud. Introducing OBJ3. In Joseph A. Goguen,

editor, *Applications of Algebraic Specification using OBJ*. Cambridge University Press, 1992.

[Goguen 1984]
Joseph A. Goguen. Parameterized programming. *IEEE Transactions on Software Engineering*, SE–10(5), September 1984.

[Goguen 1991]
Joseph A. Goguen. Types as theories. In George Michael Reed, Andrew William Roscoe, and Ralph F. Wachter, editors, *Proceedings, Topology and Category Theory in Computer Science*, pages 357–390. Oxford University Press, 1991.

[Goldberg and Robson 1983]
Adele Goldberg and David Robson. *Smalltalk-80: The Language and its Implementation*. Addison-Wesley, 1983.

[Hall 1990]
J. Anthony Hall. Using Z as a specification calculus for object-oriented systems. In [Bjørner *et al.* 1990], pages 290–318.

[Hayes 1987]
Ian J. Hayes, editor. *Specification Case Studies*. Prentice Hall, 1987.

[Iachini 1991]
P. Luigi Iachini. Operation schema iterations. In [Nicholls 1991], pages 27–49.

[ISO/IEC JTC1 SC21 N6079 1991]
ISO/IEC JTC1 SC21 N6079. Basic reference model for open distributed processing. Proposal for committee draft text, June 1991.

[ISO/IEC JTC1 SC21 WG7 N434 1991]
ISO/IEC JTC1 SC21 WG7 N434. Architectural semantics, specification techniques and formalisms. Working document, November 1991.

[Jones 1986]
Cliff B. Jones. *Systematic Software Development using VDM*. Prentice Hall, 1986.

[Lano and Breuer 1990]
Kevin C. Lano and Peter T. Breuer. From programs to Z specifications. In [Nicholls 1990], pages 46–70.

[Lano and Haughton 1991]
Kevin C. Lano and Howard Haughton. Axioms for object-oriented extensions to Z. Technical report, Programming Research Group, Oxford University Computing Laboratory, 1991.

[Lano and Haughton 1992]
Kevin C. Lano and Howard Haughton. Reasoning and refinement in object-oriented specification languages. In *Proceedings ECOOP'92*, 1992.

[Lano 1991]
Kevin C. Lano. Z++, an object-orientated extension to Z. In [Nicholls 1991], pages 151–172.

[Meira and Cavalcanti 1991]
Silvio Lemos Meira and Ana Lúcia C. Cavalcanti. Modular object oriented Z specifications. In [Nicholls 1991], pages 173–192.

[Meira and Cavalcanti 1992]
Silvio Lemos Meira and Ana Lúcia C. Cavalcanti. The MooZ specification language. Technical report, Universidade Federal de Pernambuco, Departamento de Informática, Recife - PE, 1992.

[Meira *et al.* 1991]
Silvio Lemos Meira, Ana Lúcia C. Cavalcanti, and C. S. Santos. ForMooZ: An environment for formal object-oriented specification and prototyping. Technical report, Universidade Federal de Pernambuco, Departamento de Informática, Recife - PE, 1991.

[Meira *et al.* 1992]
Silvio Lemos Meira, Ana Lúcia C. Cavalcanti, and C. S. Santos. The Unix filing system: A MooZ specification. Technical report, Universidade Federal de Pernambuco, Departamento de Informática, Recife - PE, 1992.

[Meyer 1988]
Bertrand Meyer. *Object-oriented Software Construction*. Prentice Hall, 1988.

[Meyer 1992]
Bertrand Meyer. *Eiffel: the Language*. Prentice Hall, 1992.

[Morgan 1990]
C. Carroll Morgan. *Programming from Specifications*. Prentice Hall, 1990.

[Nicholls 1990]
John E. Nicholls, editor. *Z User Workshop: Proceedings of the Fourth Annual Z User Meeting, Oxford*, Workshops in Computing. Springer Verlag, 1990.

[Nicholls 1991]
John E. Nicholls, editor. *Proceedings of the Fifth Annual Z User Meeting, Oxford*, Workshops in Computing. Springer Verlag, 1991.

[Nicholls 1992]
John E. Nicholls, editor. *Proceedings of the Sixth Annual Z User Meeting, York*, Workshops in Computing. Springer Verlag, 1992.

[Peterson 1988]
Ivars Peterson. *The Mathematical Tourist*. W. H. Freeman, 1988.

[Potter *et al.* 1991]
Ben Potter, Jane Sinclair, and David Till. *An Introduction to Formal Specification and Z*. Prentice Hall, 1991.

[Rafsanjani 1992]
G. H. B. Rafsanjani. An abstract object model for application to mapping Object-Z to C++. Internal report, British Telecom, 1992. (draft).

[Sampaio and Meira 1990]
Augusto Sampaio and Silvio Lemos Meira. Modular extensions to Z. In [Bjørner *et al.* 1990], pages 211–232.

[Schuman and Pitt 1987]
S. A. Schuman and David H. Pitt. Object-oriented subsystem specification. In L. G. L. T. Meertens, editor, *Program Specification and Transformation*, pages 313–341. North Holland, 1987.

[Schuman *et al.* 1990]
S. A. Schuman, David H. Pitt, and Paddy J. Byers. Object-oriented process specification. In C. Rattray, editor, *Specification and Verification of Concurrent Systems*, Workshops in Computing, pages 21–70. Springer Verlag, 1990.

[Shriver and Wegner 1987]
Bruce Shriver and Peter Wegner, editors. *Research Directions in Object-Oriented Programming*. MIT Press, 1987.

[Spivey 1988]
J. Michael Spivey. *Understanding Z: a specification language and its formal semantics*, volume 3 of *Cambridge Tracts in Theoretical Computer Science*. Cambridge University Press, 1988.

[Spivey 1989]
J. Michael Spivey. *The Z Notation: a Reference Manual*. Prentice Hall, 1989.

[Stanley-Smith and Cahill 1990]
C. Stanley-Smith and A. Cahill. UNIFORM: A language geared to system description and transformation. REDO Project document 2487-TN-UL-1002, University of Limerick, 1990.

[Stepney *et al.* 1992]
Susan Stepney, Rosalind Barden, and David Cooper. A survey of object orientation in Z. *IEE Software Engineering Journal*, 7(2):150–160, March 1992.

[Wegner and Zdonik 1988]
Peter Wegner and Stanley B. Zdonik. Inheritance as an incremental modification technique, or what like is and isn't like. In Stein Gjessing and Kristen Nygaard, editors, *ECOOP'88: European Conference on Object-Oriented Programming*, volume 322 of *Lecture Notes in Computer Science*, pages 55–77. Springer Verlag, 1988.

[Wegner 1987a]
Peter Wegner. Dimensions of object-based language design. *OOPSLA'87 Proceedings, ACM SIGPLAN Notices*, 22(12):168–182, 1987.

[Wegner 1987b]

Peter Wegner. The object-oriented classification paradigm. In [Shriver and Wegner 1987].

[Whysall and McDermid 1991a]

Peter J. Whysall and John A. McDermid. An approach to object oriented specification using Z. In [Nicholls 1991], pages 193–215.

[Whysall and McDermid 1991b]

Peter J. Whysall and John A. McDermid. Object oriented specification and refinement. In Joseph M. Morris and Roger C. Shaw, editors, *4th Refinement Workshop*, Workshops in Computing, pages 150–184. Springer Verlag, 1991.

[Wills 1991]

Alan Wills. Capsules and types in Fresco: Program validation in Smalltalk. In [America 1991], pages 59–76.

[Woodcock and Loomes 1988]

James C. P. Woodcock and Martin Loomes. *Software Engineering Mathematics*. Pitman, 1988.

[Woodcock 1989]

James C. P. Woodcock. Structuring specifications in Z. *IEE Software Engineering Journal*, 4(1):51–66, 1989.

[Zimmer 1990]

J. A. Zimmer. Restructuring for style. *Software—Practice and Experience*, 20(4):365–389, April 1990.

Published in 1990

AI and Cognitive Science '89, Dublin City
University, Eire, 14–15 September 1989
A. F. Smeaton and G. McDermott (Eds.)

**Specification and Verification of Concurrent
Systems,** University of Stirling, Scotland,
6–8 July 1988
C. Rattray (Ed.)

Semantics for Concurrency, Proceedings of the
International BCS-FACS Workshop, Sponsored
by Logic for IT (S.E.R.C.), University of
Leicester, UK, 23–25 July 1990
M. Z. Kwiatkowska, M. W. Shields and
R. M. Thomas (Eds.)

Functional Programming, Glasgow 1989,
Proceedings of the 1989 Glasgow Workshop,
Fraserburgh, Scotland, 21–23 August 1989
K. Davis and J. Hughes (Eds.)

Persistent Object Systems, Proceedings of the
Third International Workshop, Newcastle,
Australia, 10–13 January 1989
J. Rosenberg and D. Koch (Eds.)

Z User Workshop, Oxford, 1989, Proceedings of
the Fourth Annual Z User Meeting, Oxford,
15 December 1989
J. E. Nicholls (Ed.)

**Formal Methods for Trustworthy Computer
Systems (FM89),** Halifax, Canada,
23–27 July 1989
Dan Craigen (Editor) and Karen Summerskill
(Assistant Editor)

Security and Persistence, Proceedings of the
International Workshop on Computer
Architecture to Support Security and Persistence
of Information, Bremen, West Germany,
8–11 May 1990
John Rosenberg and J. Leslie Keedy (Eds.)

Printing: Weihert-Druck GmbH, Darmstadt
Binding: Buchbinderei Schäffer, Grünstadt